Integrated Economic Accounting

Integrated Economic Accounting

Theory and Applications to
National, Real, and
Financial Economic
Planning

Hector Correa
University of Pittsburgh

Lexington Books
D. C. Heath and Company
Lexington, Massachusetts
Toronto

Library of Congress Cataloging in Publication Data
Correa, Héctor.
    Integrated economic accounting.
    Includes index.
    1. Accounting. 2. Interindustry economics. 3. National in-
come—Accounting. 4. Economic policy. I. Title.
HF5635.C794   657   76-17445
ISBN 0-669-00779-X

Published simultaneously in Canada

Printed in the United States of America

International Standard Book Number: 0-669-00779-X

Library of Congress Catalog Card Number: 76-17445

Contents

List of Tables

Acknowledgments

My sincere thanks go to Professor Gene Gruver, Department of Economics, University of Pittsburgh, for the valuable comments on several aspects of this book and to several groups of students, both at Tulane University and in the Graduate School of Public and International Affairs at the University of Pittsburgh. They helped me on the long road that led from the initial conception of the approach used in this book to its completion. In particular, my thanks go to Mr. David Mora, who contributed in the reformulation of the national accounts of the U.S.A., to Mr. and Mrs. Horacio Braslavsky, who prepared the first numerical example of the generalized equation of exchange, to Mr. Leonel Fletes, who developed the method for estimating the national transactions table explained in Chapter 10, and to Mr. Nguyen Tan Trieu, who prepared the computations in Chapter 12.

Special thanks also go to my wife, Mrs. Virginia Correa, who, far beyond the call of duty, corrects my English and prepares first drafts, in addition to being a loving mother to six rambunctious children; and to the secretarial personnel of the Graduate School of Public and International Affairs, who have typed several copies of the manuscript.

Glossary of Abbreviations

Bk	Bank(s)
DNTT	Detailed national transactions tables
FFS	Flow of funds statement
GEE	Generalized equation of exchange
Gov	Government
GNP	Gross national product
Hh	Household(s)
HL	Homeland
Ind	Industry
IOS	Input-output statement
IOT	Input-output table
IPS	Income and product statement
Mf	Manufacturer(s)
NDNTT	Nondetailed national transactions tables
NEC	Not elsewhere classified
NIP	National income and product
NTT	National transactions tables
RTS	Real transactions statement
RW	Rest of the world
SVS	Saving and investment statement

**Integrated Economic
Accounting**

1 Introduction

The object of this book is to present micro- and macro-accounting as a logical unit. Chapters 2 and 3 contain the basic ideas of micro-accounting. The accounting processes of a nonproducing economic unit, such as a household or a store, are discussed in Chapter 2. Chapter 3 demonstrates the accounting process of a producing economic unit, that is, the concepts presented in Chapter 2 are extended to include the principles of cost accounting.

After the basic ideas of micro-accounting have been presented, the following five chapters show their application to economic units representing the main sectors into which an economy can be divided: households, industry, finance, government and rest of the world. These applications emphasize the fact that the same principles are used for all the units. It is only the names of the accounts that change. In these five chapters, actual U.S. sector accounts are used for illustration purposes.

In addition, in each of the first seven chapters, a complete example (called the *example for the chapter*) is presented. The object of these examples is to facilitate the understanding of the material and to provide raw materials, together with the U.S. sector accounts, for the construction of the macro-accounting statements.

The study of macro-accounting begins with the derivation of the *national balance statement* from the balance statements of each of the sectors in which the economy has been divided. From the national balance statement, the values of national wealth and national capital are obtained.

Next, a *national transactions table* is constructed on the basis of a systematic summary of the transactions statements of all the micro-units representing sectors of the economy. This table is used as the starting point for all the macro-accounting statements.

The first statement derived from the national transactions table is a rectification and generalization of Fisher's Equation of Exchange. The importance of this reformulation of Fisher's Equation is that the equation constitutes the core of the quantity theory of money. It integrates both the real and the financial aspects of an economy.

Next, statements dealing only with the financial or the real aspects of an economy, but not with both, are derived from the national transactions table. The first group includes the *national flow of funds statement*. The chapter dealing with this statement presents the methods that have been

1

developed to forecast the complete statement when forecasts of tangible assets are available.

Finally, the statements reflecting only the real or net worth aspects of the transactions of the different economic sectors are derived from the national transactions table. These statements, ranked in order of consolidation, are *the input/output statement, the national income and product statement* and the *gross saving and investment statement*. In the chapter dealing with the input/output statement, the methods available for the analysis and forecast of input/output tables are presented.

The book ends with two chapters presenting models for forecasting and planning the real and financial aspects of an economy. In the first of these chapters, models with one production sector are considered. In the second, the production sector is characterized by an inter-industry model of any number of sectors.

The integration of micro- and macro-accounting used in this book will be helpful to students of accounting, to specialists in micro-accounting of any one sector, and to economists interested in macro-accounting. To the specialists in one sector of micro-accounting, it will provide a better idea of the scope of the techniques they use. To students and professionals of economics who struggle with nonsystematic presentations of bank, rest of the world, macro-flow of funds, and macro-real accounting, the possibility of deriving all these accounts from the same basic principles and of seeing them as parts of a single structure will be useful.

Finally, economists, whether interested in theory or applications, have expressed the urgent need for instruments that integrate the real and financial aspects of an economy. They will find the last two chapters of this book particularly helpful.

2

Principles of Micro-Accounting: The Accounting Process of Non-Production Units

2.1 Economic Dimensions—Stocks and Flows

Only an intuitive introduction to the idea of dimension will be presented here. For a more formal presentation, see the studies mentioned in the reference section.

The basic property of two quantities of the same dimension is that when they are added together the total is of the same dimension as the addends. For example, the number of students in one class can be added to that of another class to obtain the total number of students, because the two numbers are of the same dimension. However, the number of men in a class cannot be added to the number of women in the same class to obtain a total in terms of men or women. In this case, the dimensions are different.

In economics, four groups of primary dimensions can be identified:

1. commodities, including claims against third persons
2. money
3. time
4. utility or satisfaction.

It should be observed that each of these four groups includes several dimensions. Each good has its own dimension. Cars and planes cannot be added together. Money also includes several dimensions. Practically all the elements considered in accounting are in a money dimension and thus can be added together.

One or several of the primary dimensions appear either implicitly or explicitly in the definition of any economic variable. *When only one primary dimension appears, the variable is a stock.* For instance, the number of tons of wheat and the total value of money in circulation are stocks. Frequently the term "stock" is reserved for variables in any of the primary dimensions except time. However, this does not have to be the case. *A flow variable has a secondary dimension, that is its dimensions are a combination of two of the primary ones.* For example, income per unit of time is a flow variable. Again in this case, the term "flow variables" is frequently restricted to those that have time as a second dimension.

3

2.2 Main Accounting Statements—The Accounting Process

Accounting involves the systematic recording, summarization, and interpretation of the economic activities of an economic unit during a fixed period of time called the *accounting period*.

It will be assumed here that the accounting period continues from date t to date $t + 1$. It will also be assumed that the study of all the economic units begins at date t. All the information needed about the economic units at date t is known.

The main accounting summaries of the economic activities of a unit can be classified in two groups:

1. those dealing with stocks at a fixed date. *The balance statements* are the main ones in this group. At least two balance statements are prepared during the accounting period, one at the beginning and one at the end of the period. From a purely formal point of view, accounting is the process of passing from the initial to the final balance, taking into consideration the economic operations of the accounting units which have taken place during that time.
2. those dealing with the economic flows over the accounting period. The *transactions statement* and the *income statement* are the main ones in this group. Each of these statements presents modifications of the initial balance. When appropriately added to the initial balance, the final one is obtained.

Each of these statements can be expressed as a mathematical identity. For this reason, the terms "accounting statements", "identities" and "equations" will be used as synonyms. A detailed description of each of these accounting statements and their interpretation is presented in the following sections.

2.3 The Balance Equation

2.3.1 The Equation

It was noted earlier that during the accounting period at least two balance statements are prepared for the economic unit. The description to be presented here is applicable to both of them.

The balance equation is

$$A_t + T_t = B_t + N_t \qquad (2.1)$$

where A = tangible assets, T = financial assets, B = liabilities, N = net worth, and t as a subscript denotes date in time. Each of the elements in the balance equation will be defined here.

Assets are items of value owned by an economic unit. They are usually classified as:

1. real or tangible assets such as plant, equipment, and inventories
2. financial assets or claims. These are rights to receive, or claims of the economic unit being studied on another. Examples are currency, deposits, and accounts receivable.

Liabilities are debts or obligations of the economic unit being studied to pay money or other assets or to render services to another economic unit. It should be understood that the liabilities of one unit are among the financial assets of another unit.

Net Worth is, by definition, the difference between assets and liabilities. It represents the equity of the owner or owners of the assets. This definition of net worth is valid whether the owner is a real person or a legal person, as in the case of a corporation. The previous observations show that net worth, from this point of view, is only a monetary value without any real counterpart.

Since net worth is defined as the difference between assets and liabilities, the balance equation *always* holds. It is an identity.

An example of a balance sheet is presented in Table 2–1.

2.3.2 Detailed Study of Assets and Liabilities

This section will first present a detailed description and some examples of financial assets and liabilities. The nature of financial assets and liabilities seems to be more difficult to understand than that of real assets. Next, characteristics common to both real and financial assets will be presented and, finally, the economic function of the assets will be described.

Description of Financial Assets and Liabilities. The most common financial asset and liability is money, either in the form of currency or of demand deposits. A detailed description of money should not be required here.

The most commonly known nonmonetary financial assets and liabilities are loans made by one accounting unit to another. Such loans are financial assets for the unit making the loan and liabilities for the unit receiving it, since it is implicit in the idea of a loan that the accounting unit receiving it will repay the loan to the unit making it. With few exceptions,

Table 2–1
Example of a Balance Sheet (*December 31, ...*)

Assets		Liabilities and Net Worth	
Tangible Assets (A)		*Liabilities (B)*	
Equipment	100,000	Notes Payable	35,000
Buildings	50,000		
Land	10,000		
Inventories	45,000	*Net Worth (N)*	185,000
Financial Assets (T)			
Cash and deposits	15,000		
Total	220,000	Total	220,000

at least in most occidental countries, the purpose of the unit making a loan is to receive interest. [a]

It is useful to interpret a loan as the purchase of a right that the lender makes to the receiver. The payment of a loan is the purchase the receiver makes of this same right to the lender. A document specifies the details of the rights bought and sold, in particular the date and conditions of the first and second sale purchases.

It is implicit in these observations that lender and receiver are clearly specified and identified in the right bought or sold. This is the case for some types of financial documents, but not for others. Many financial documents can be sold by the lender to a third party, as well as to the receiver. Bonds issued by governments or by private enterprises are perhaps the most common form of a financial asset that can be sold to third parties.

In summary, nonmonetary financial assets and liabilities can be subdivided on the basis of whether or not they individualize both buyer and seller, and whether they have a maturity or repurchase date.

Characteristics of Assets. All assets, whether real or financial, have two basic characteristics: a) they are *stores of value* and b) they have some *liquidity*. These two characteristics will be described here.

Assets have been defined as items having value, that is, they store value or are stores of value. It is important to observe that, while this characteristic is used in the definition of money, it is not typical of it. Actually, the fact that it is a store of value does not differentiate money from any

---

[a] In some Moslem countries it is possible to receive interest-free loans because interest is forbidden in the Koran. In such cases the principal lender is the state.

other asset and, in many cases, other assets are better stores of value than money. This is so because, under inflation, the value of money decreases while that of other assets increases.

Another property characteristic of all assets is liquidity. One asset is more liquid than another if it is more certainly realizable (exchanged for other assets that are needed at that time) at short notice without loss. Money is fully liquid in the sense that it can be exchanged immediately for any other asset. Liquidity is important because the fully liquid asset can be used as a means of payment. Liquidity is a much more typical characteristic of money, because money is usually the only fully liquid asset. However, some other assets can be more liquid than money, for example, cigarette currency in immediate post World War I Germany.

Another characteristic that is largely reserved to money is that of being the *unit of account*. This means that the values of other assets are expressed in terms of money or that money is the measure of value. The existence of a unit of account makes accounting possible. However, the fact that money is not a completely stable measure of value (for example, its value being reduced by inflation) is the cause of some of the most difficult problems in accounting. These problems will not be discussed in this book.

Functions of the Assets. The functions performed by the assets in an economic unit are a consequence of their characteristics. This means that all assets perform similar functions but in different degrees and combinations.

It is said that assets perform a *running function* when they satisfy the needs of current operations of an accounting unit.

Examples of tangible assets in a running function are clothing, furniture, and silverware for households, and equipment, machinery, and implements for firms, banks, and other financial institutions and governments. Money also performs a running function when it is used to pay grocery bills and salaries and to maintain legal reserves. The property of money in this case is that of being a means of payment. Money held for its running function is called transactions money. Finally, credit open to maintain a trade is an example of a nonmoney financial asset used for a running function. (For example, the usual credit of car dealers has a running function for them.)

Assets satisfy a *reserve function* when they are held for emergencies that may arise in the future. Spare parts are tangible assets used for reserve. They are held for specific emergencies, in the same way that a spare tire can be used as reserves for unspecified emergencies as long as they store value and are more or less liquid. This means that, from the point of view of reserves, money clearly has an advantage over the other financial assets. Money held as reserve is called precautionary money.

Assets perform an *investment function* when they are held for the sake of the profit which they are expected to earn. Any tangible asset held because its value is expected to increase in the future performs an investment function. Nonmonetary financial assets perform better than money as investment assets if their prices do not decrease. For example, if the price of certain shares of stock is $100 and the return on these shares is $5 per year, then these shares of stock are performing better as investment assets than $100 held in cash or in a deposit account without interest. However, if the return is maintained but the selling price is reduced to $90, the shares did not perform as well as money. In this case, the return of money, being zero in terms of money, is above that of the share, that is, minus five. However, the return of money, measured in terms of the value of the share, is positive. Money held in the expectation of a price reduction is called speculative money.

2.3.3 Valuation of the Variables in the Balance Equation

General Principles. All the variables in the balance statement, and in all its modifications to be described here, are evaluated in monetary terms.

The monetary value given by an accounting unit to the variables in the balance statement is, to begin with, equal to the amount of money paid or received by the tangible and financial assets and liabilities represented by these variables. After an initial transaction involving assets and liabilities, their accounting values can be changed by means of revaluations. During these revaluations an attempt is made to give the assets and liabilities the values they would have if a transaction involving them took place at a later date. In other words, an attempt is made to give them their current market values.

Valuation of Tangible Assets. The estimation of the monetary value of a tangible asset, whether for an initial transaction or for a revaluation, does not present any conceptual problem. The value is equal to the price of the asset multiplied by its quantity. The problems in specifying the price that should be used, particularly when an asset is revalued without an actual transaction, will not be discussed here.

It is useful to observe at this point that the belief that price and quantity of tangible assets are well-defined entities is somewhat misleading. The unit of quantity and, as a consequence, unitary price are completely arbitrary. This is so even when no changes in quality are considered. For example, a quantity of wheat can be measured in bushels, kilos, tons, etc., and a unitary price can correspond to each of these units. Also, to use one car as a unit might be very misleading when cars of different qualities are being considered.

Valuation of Financial Assets and Liabilities. Conceptually, the initial valuation and the revaluation of financial assets and liabilities are somewhat more difficult. One reason for this is that, in transactions involving financial claims and liabilities, what purchaser and seller usually give and expect to receive is money. In addition, the amount of money that the purchaser of a financial asset expects to receive on a future date and that the seller is willing to give usually is larger than the amount that the purchaser initially pays for a claim. Finally, as will be seen in more detail later, at least the part of the money called interest that the purchaser receives from the seller of a claim is not recorded in the balance statement. It appears only in transactions and income statements, to be studied later.

It follows from the previous statements that the valuation of financial claims involves the integration of the initial payment from the buyer to the seller of a claim, that is, the loan, and of the future payments from the seller to the buyer on the specified dates, that is, interest or profits and, when applicable, principal. In addition, the way that the different qualities involved appear in the accounts has to be specified.

The integration of the different quantities mentioned is made under the assumption of no risk. The amount paid by the purchaser (lender) of a claim to its seller is equal to the present value of the payments that the seller agrees to make in the future.

More specifically, if a loan of L dollars at an annual interest rate of i is made for n years, this means that the buyer gives (lends) to the seller L dollars and expects to receive iL dollars each year for n years and, finally, L dollars again the nth year. The present value of this sequence of payment is

$$P(L, i, n) = \sum_{t=1}^{n} -\frac{iL}{(1 + i)^t} + \frac{L}{(1 + i)^n}$$

that is, using the formula for the sum of a geometric projection,

$$P(L, i, n) = \frac{L(1 + i)^n - 1}{(1 + i)^n} + \frac{L}{(1 + i)^n}$$

which expression is equal to L.

It can also be easily verified that if $m \leq n$ periods have passed and, as a consequence, m interest payments of L have been made, the present value of the loan remains equal to L. The reason for this is that in the formula above the exponent n is replaced with the exponent $n - m$.

So far it has been assumed that the sequence of future receipts and payments is certain for both the buyer and the seller. If further receipts and payments are uncertain, the probabilities that the buyer and seller attach to the future payments and receipts would have to be included in the computation of present value. This present value could be computed with a formula similar to that used to specify the value of a life insurance policy. The probabilities of surviving are replaced with the subjective probabilities that the payments will be made.

In the case of uncertain loans like those described here, if the amount of the loan L, the future returns F, the market rate of discount, and the time for repayment (if specified) are known, it is possible to estimate the cost of uncertainty. This is equal to the difference $P(F, i, n) - L$ between the present value of the future payments F at the discount rate i minus the amount paid for them, that is, L. The present value will tend to be larger than L to compensate for the uncertainty of the lender.

To complete the study of the valuation of financial assets and liabilities, some observations will be made on the effect of changes of the future return expected with a financial claim. In this respect the following observations can be made:

1. If the amount and time sequence of future returns is fixed by contract, the present value of those returns will tend to decrease if the rate of discount increases. The reason for this is obvious if one observes the formulas for present value given previously.

2. If the amount of future returns or their certainty increases (decreases), while the rate of discount remains constant, present value tends to increase (decrease).

Similarly, an increase (decrease) in the returns of claims can be identified with a change in the rate of discount.

The change in value of claims can be computed using as a starting point the present values $P_{i_t} = P(L, i_t, n)$ and $P_{i_o} = p(L, i_o, n)$ computed with the current discount rate i_t and the discount rate on the base date. Different indices of change would be

$$P_{i_t}/P_{i_o} \quad \text{and} \quad (P_{i_t} - P_{i_o}) \, P_{io}.$$

It should be observed that in order to evaluate the change in value of claims being traded in the capital markets it is sufficient to compare the amounts paid for them. This conclusion follows from the fact that

$$L_t = P_{i_t} \quad \text{and} \quad L_o = P_{io}.$$

If the information required to evaluate the cost of uncertainty is available for the cases in which both the discount rates i_0 and i_t are used, it is possible to estimate the effect on the value of a loan of both the change in the discount rate and the cost of uncertainty.

Value of Assets in the Balance Equation. In order to emphasize some earlier observations on the value of assets in the balance equation, they are repeated here.

Assets, whether tangible or financial, are valued in the balance equation in monetary units. The amounts appearing in this equation are initially equal to the amount paid for them. This means, in the case of financial assets and liabilities, that the amount appearing in the balance equation is equal to the present value of the future payments that the seller of a claim should make to its purchaser. This present value includes both the influence of the discount rate evaluated under conditions of certainty, and the cost of uncertainty with respect to future payments.

2.4 The Transactions Equation

2.4.1 Definition of Transactions

A transaction is any operation of the accounting unit that affects the elements of the balance equation. Whatever the modification of the elements of the balance equation, the equation itself, that is, the equality between the left and right sides of the equation, is always maintained. In order to do this, the value of net worth can be modified. This means that the balance equation

$$A_j + T_j = B_j + N_j \tag{2.2}$$

up to and including transaction j, changes to the balance equation

$$A_{j+1} + T_{j+1} = B_{j+1} + N_{j+1}$$

after transaction $j + 1$.

From the balance equations before and after the transaction, equation (2.3) can be obtained:

$$\Delta A_{j+1} + \Delta T_{j+1} = \Delta B_{j+1} + \Delta N_{j+1} \tag{2.3}$$

where the notation ΔA_{j+1} means increments of A between transactions j and $j + 1$ or $\Delta A_{j+1} = A_{j+1} - A_j$. The other symbols have a comparable meaning. The increments show the influence of the operation of the accounting unit on the balance equation; that is, equation (2.3) describes the transaction itself. For any transaction, equality is maintained in equation (2.3) because it is the difference between two equations.

Examples of Transactions.

Example 1. The accounting unit purchases inventories for $15,000 of which it pays $5,000 in cash and leaves the remainder on credit.

$$\Delta A = +15,000 \text{ due to change in inventories}$$

$$\Delta T = -5,000 \text{ due to payment in cash}$$

$$\Delta B = +10,000 \text{ due to increase in liabilities}$$

The transaction equation is

$$\text{inventories} - \text{cash} = \text{liabilities}$$

$$15,000 - 5,000 = 10,000$$

Example 2. The accounting unit borrows $15,000 from the bank, signing a promissory note for the amount.

$$\Delta T = +15,000 \text{ due to change in cash available}$$

$$\Delta B = +15,000 \text{ due to change in notes payable}$$

The equation of the transaction is

$$\text{cash} = \text{notes payable}$$

$$15,000 = 15,000$$

A set of transactions for a household (Hh) are presented here as the example for Chapter 2:

1. Hh purchases, for immediate consumption, manufacturer's (Mf) goods for $6730, pays $6000 in check, $730 cash.
2. Hh pays bank (Bk) $400 for services provided by payment, $300 check, $100 cash.
3. Hh receives (a) $1485 as profits from Mf. Payment $1000 in check, $485 in cash; (b) $5370 as wages from Mf. Payment $5000 in check, $370 in cash. Checks deposited immediately.
4. Hh buys securities from (a) Mf for $300 paid with check; (b) Bk for $200 paid in cash.
5. Hh receives payment of $250 from Mf for standing debt. Payment $200 in check, $50 in cash.

6. Hh receives payments from Bk of (a) \$600 as wages. Payment increasing Hh deposits; (b) \$875 as distributed profits. Payment \$800 increasing Hh deposits, remainder in cash.

2.4.2 Recording of Transactions

The transaction equation (2.3) can be used to explain the debit and credit rules used to record transactions as a simple matter of mathematical notation. It should be observed that the terms "debit" and "credit" are simply another way of saying "plus" or "minus." To avoid confusion it should be emphasized that this does not imply that debit denotes +, and credit −, or vice versa. The fact is that a positive increment of assets is arbitrarily called a debit, while negative increments or reductions of assets are called credits. For the change in sign needed to go from one side of equation (2.3) to the other, it follows that negative increments of liabilities or net worth must be called debits, and positive increments, credits. These observations are summarized in Table 2–2.

Using these rules, the transactions in Examples 1 and 2 in Section 2.4.1 are recorded in Table 2–3.

The previous observations made with respect to debit and credit rules are maintained if it is assumed that the transaction equation is written

$$\Delta A - \Delta B - \Delta N = 0 \tag{2.4}$$

instead of in the form used in equation (2.3) or with the meaning given to debits and credits in Table 2–2, as

debits to assets

+ debits to liabilities

+ debits to net worth

− credits to assets $\hspace{2cm}$ (2.5)

− credits to liabilities

− credits to net worth

equals zero

The most commonly used way to record transactions is to write all the debits in one column and all the credits in another column, with total debits equal to total credits; that is, using the equality implied in equation (2.5). This method will be avoided here because it obscures the basic principles of accounting.

Table 2–2
Debit and Credit Rules

$\Delta Assets$		=	$\Delta Liabilities$		+	$\Delta Net\ Worth$	
+Debit	−Credit		−Debit	+Credit		−Debit	+Credit

Another term frequently used in place of "debits" is "uses of funds," and for "credits," "sources of funds." History or tradition is the main reason for these alternative terms, as it is for the original ones. However, it is possible to rationalize the new terms by observing that many and perhaps most of the transactions imply an exchange of physical or financial resources between two accounting units. The unit that gives away the physical or financial assets first records this part of the transaction with credits and then receives in exchange some financial assets such as cash or an account receivable that are recorded as debits. These take the generic name of "funds." As a result, the credits are a source of the funds. These funds are kept in the form of cash or other financial assets, that is, they are used in those forms.

Similarly, the unit that receives the assets records that part of the transaction with debits and is using its funds in the assets received. The reduction of the financial assets paid in exchange for the assets received is a credit or a source of the funds used.

The recording of the set of transactions in the example for Chapter 2 is presented in Table 2–4.

2.4.3 Transactions Affecting Net Worth

The recording of the transactions affecting net worth has some special characteristics. Some of these will be explained here and others later on, while studying the accounting process of production firms. It should be clear that these transactions play an important role in the specification of changes for better or for worse in the economic conditions of an accounting unit. This follows from the fact that net worth is a description of the economic condition of the unit. As a result, it is necessary to pay special attention to this statement.

The fact that no specific asset, tangible or financial, can be assigned to net worth helps to identify transactions affecting it. In other words, net worth is affected when there is a transaction that cannot be described completely by changes in specific assets or liabilities. However, if such a transaction takes place, it is not recorded as balancing the changes in assets and/or liabilities with a change in net worth as such. Rather, accounts

Table 2–3
Records of Examples 1 and 2 of Section 2.4.1

Transaction	Concept	Tangible Assets		Financial Assets		Liabilities		Net Worth	
		+Debit	−Credit	+Debit	−Credit	−Debit	+Credit	−Debit	+Credit
a	Inventories	15,000							
	Cash				5,000				
	Accounts Payable						10,000		
b	Cash			15,000					
	Notes Payable						15,000		

Table 2–4
Example for Chapter 2: Recording of the Transactions

	Tangible Assets		Financial Assets		Liabilities		Net Worth	
	+Debit	−Credit	+Debit	−Credit	−Debit	+Credit	−Debit	+Credit
1. Consumption Mf							6,730	
Deposits Mf				6,000				
Cash				730				
2. Use Bk							400	
Deposits Bk				300				
Cash				100				
3a. Profits Mf								1,485
Deposits			1,000					
Cash			485					
3b. Wages Mf								5,370
Deposits			5,000					
Cash			370					
4a. Securities Mf			300					
Deposits				300				
4b. Securities Bk			200					
Cash				200				
5. Accounts Receivable Mf				250				
Deposits			200					
Cash			50					
6a. Wages Bk								600
Deposits			600					
6b. Profits Bk								875
Deposits			800					
Cash			75					
Total			9,080	7,880			7,130	8,330

are introduced to describe the transactions. Net worth itself, and under that name, is never modified during the accounting period. The accounts introduced to describe changes in net worth during the accounting period are used at the end of the period to evaluate the total change in net worth. The main reason for this is the need to have a detailed description of the changes in net worth, not only of their net value. In this way it is possible to identify the reason for these changes.

The preceding observations can be explained with the following example: Consider a purely commercial firm, that is, one that does not produce the goods it sells. A transaction affecting net worth could be, in this case, the payment of wages. To be more specific, let the transaction be payment of $5000 in cash as wages. It is clear in this case that the reduction of cash cannot be balanced with any change in assets or liabilities. As a result, net worth is affected. However, as observed, in the recording of the transaction the reduction of cash is not balanced with a reduction of net worth, but with the reduction of a specific account representing net worth, in this case, wages. In summary, the transaction in this case is recorded as in Table 2–5.

The main transactions affecting net worth are those referring to (a) income received in the case of households; (b) distribution of profits, payment of wages and interests, depreciation, and sales in the case of purely commercial firms; (c) distribution of profits and sales in the case of producing firms (the reasons for the difference between commercial and producing firms will be explained later); and (d) taxes received and payments for goods produced in the case of government.

A particularly important transaction affecting net worth is the sale of goods by a commercial or producing firm. This type of transaction actually involves two operations on the part of the selling accounting unit: (a) the actual sale and the reception of a payment balancing assets; and (b) the reduction of assets in the amount of the goods sold. The recording of these two operations can be explained with an example (see Table 2–6): A firm sells goods for $8000 cash, from an inventory bought for $5000.

It should be observed that two accounts affecting net worth are used to record a sale: (a) the sale itself, which increases net worth as a consequence of the payment for the goods sold; and (b) the reduction of net worth due to the reduction of goods available and recorded as cost of goods sold.

In Table 2–4 it can be observed that parts of transactions 1, 2, 3a, 3b, 6a, and 6b in Section 2.4.1 affect net worth.

2.4.4 The Transactions Statement

The transactions statement is a summary of all the transactions performed by an accounting unit during the accounting period. It consists of the ele-

Table 2–5
Accounting for Transactions Affecting Net Worth (Wages)

	$\Delta Assets$		=	$\Delta Liabilities$	+		$\Delta Net\ Worth$	
	+Debit	−Credit		−Debit	+Credit		−Debit	+Credit
Cash	5,000							
Wages							5,000	

Table 2–6
Recording for Transactions Affecting Net Worth (Sale of Goods)

	$\Delta Assets$		=	$\Delta Liabilities$	+		$\Delta Net\ Worth$	
	+Debit	−Credit		−Debit	+Credit		−Debit	+Credit
Sales								8,000
Cash	8,000							
Inventories		5,000						
Cost of Goods							5,000	

ments of each transaction affecting a specific account, which are added together, maintaining the distinction between debits and credits. Table 2–7 shows the preparation of the transactions statement for the household for which transactions were presented at the end of Section 2.4.1. The transactions statement consists of the totals of debits and credits for each account. The statement for the example for this chapter appears in Table 2–8.

Using symbols, there is no way to distinguish between an individual transaction equation and the equation corresponding to the transactions statement. Both have the general form presented in equation (2.3). However, in the case of the transactions statement, the change in net worth is recorded with specific net worth accounts, such as consumption, profits, and wages. With this, the transactions statement of a household can be shown in symbols as

$$\Delta A_{t+1} + \Delta T_{t+1} = \Delta B_{t+1} + W_{t+1} + P_{t+1} - C_{t+1} \tag{2.6}$$

where W denotes wages, P denotes profits, and C consumption. The meanings of the other symbols have been explained. In the case of a com-

Table 2–7
Example for Chapter 2: Preparation of the Transactions Statement

Cash			Deposits		
Transactions	*Debit*	*Credit*	*Transactions*	*Debit*	*Credit*
1		730	1		6,000
2		100	2		300
3a	485		3a	1,000	
3b	370		3b	5,000	
4b		200	4a		300
5	50		5	200	
6b	75		6a	600	
			6b	800	
Total	980	1,030	*Total*	7,600	6,600

Securities			Consumption		
Transactions	*Debit*	*Credit*	*Transactions*	*Debit*	*Credit*
4a	300		1	6,730	
4b	200		2	400	
5		250			
Total	500	250	*Total*	7130	

Profits			Wages		
Transactions	*Debit*	*Credit*	*Transactions*	*Debit*	*Credit*
3a		1,485	3b		5,370
6b		875	6a		600
Total		2,360	*Total*		5,970

Table 2–8
Example for Chapter 2: Transactions Statement

	Debits	*Credits*
Cash	980	1,030
Deposits	7,600	6,600
Securities	500	250
Net Worth		
Consumption	7,130	
Profits		2,360
Wages		5,970
Total	16,210	16,210

mercial firm, the transactions statement takes the form

$$\Delta A_{t+1} + \Delta T_{t+1} = \Delta B_{t+1} + pQ_{t+1} - wL_{t+1} - iB_{t+1} - rA_{t+1} - K_{t+1}$$

(2.7)

where p = price of goods, Q = quantity of goods, pQ = sales, w = wage rate, L = number of man hours, wL = total wages paid, i = interest rate, iB = total interest paid, r = depreciation rate, rA = total depreciation, and K cost of goods sold. In this equation it is assumed that no profits have been distributed.

It should be clear that for the summary of the transactions, as for each transaction, the interpretation of sources and uses of funds is valid. For this reason, this summary (with some lines modified) is also called the flow of funds equation.

2.5 The Income Equation

A third step in the accounting process is the preparation of the income and product statement of an accounting unit. This statement is prepared from only a part of the transaction's statement, the part dealing with net worth. This explains why, using as a starting point the transactions equation or its summary, that is, mathematical identities, it is possible to obtain positive or negative income or product.

Actually, the income and product statement can be considered simply as a detailed presentation of the debits and credits to the net worth of an accounting unit. The income or product of a unit is the positive or negative difference

$$\Delta N = \text{credits to net worth} - \text{debits to net worth}$$

The income and product statement, when ΔN is positive, is usually written

$$\text{debits to net worth} + \Delta N = \text{credits to net worth}$$

When ΔN is negative, it appears on the right-hand side of the preceding equation. With this, the customary equality between debits and credits is maintained.

More specifically, it follows from equation (2.6) that the income statement for households has the form

$$\Delta N_{t+1} = W_{t+1} + P_{t+1} - C_{t+1}$$

(2.8)

and from equation (2.7) the income statement for a commercial unit takes the form:

Table 2–9
Summary of the Accounting Process

(1)	Initial Balance Debit Uses (2)	Credit Sources (3)	Transactions Statement Debit Uses (4)	Credit Sources (5)	Income Statement Debit Uses (6)	Credit Sources (7)	Final Balance Debit Uses (8)	Credit Sources (9)
Assets								
Tangible	A_t		ΔA_{t+1}				A_{t+1}	
Depreciation				rA_{t+1}				rA_{t+1}
Financial								
Cash	M_t		ΔM_{t+1}				M_{t+1}	
Deposits	D_t		ΔD_{t+1}				D_{t+1}	
Liabilities		B_t		ΔB_{t+1}				B_{t+1}
Net Worth		N_t						N_t
Wages			wL_{t+1}		wL_{t+1}			
Interest			iB_{t+1}		iB_{t+1}			
Depreciation			rA_{t+1}		rA_{t+1}			
Cost of Goods			K_{t+1}		K_{t+1}			
Profit & Loss					f_{t+1}			f_{t+1}
Sales				pQ_{t+1}		pQ_{t+1}		

$$f_{t+1} = \Delta N_{t+1} = pQ_{t+1} - wL_{t+1} - iB_{t+1} - rA_{t+1} - K_{t+1} \qquad (2.9)$$

where f denotes income or profits. (In equation (2.9), as in equation (2.7), it is assumed that no profits have been distributed.)

The income statement for the household in the example for this chapter can be read easily in Table 2–8 and will not be presented in a separate table.

2.6 The Accounting Process

As mentioned earlier, the accounting process is the transition from the initial to the final balance, by means of the transactions and income equations.

In Table 2–9 the initial and final balances, the transactions statement, and the income statement for a commercial firm are integrated. Perhaps the only aspect of this table that needs explanation is the shift of profits from the debit side of the income statement to the credit side of the first balance. This shift simply means that f_{t+1} is replaced rather than

$$pQ_{t+1} - wL_{t+1} - iB_{t+1} - rA_{t+1} - K_{t+1}$$

in equation (2.7).

References

Boulding, K., Economics and Accounting: The Uncongenial Twins, in Baxter, W. T., and Davidson, S., *Studies in Accounting Theory* (Homewood, Ill.: Irwin, 1962).

Hicks, J., *Critical Essays in Monetary Theory* (Oxford: Clarendon Press, 1967).

Mathews, R., *Accounting for Economists* (Chapters 1 to 6) (London: Angus and Robertson, 1969).

Powelson, J., *Economic Accounting* (Chapter 2) New York: McGraw-Hill, 1955).

3

Principles of Micro-Accounting: The Accounting Process of Production Units

3.1 A Preliminary Comparison between the Accounting Processes of Production and Nonproduction Units

In Chapter 2 the accounting process was described as beginning with a balance statement. Then transactions that modified some elements of this statement were performed, recorded according to certain rules, and, finally, summarized in the transactions statement. This summary makes it possible to evaluate the income statement or change in net worth, and when properly added to the initial balance it shows the final balance of the accounting unit over the accounting period.

The steps mentioned are also performed in the case of a production unit. Each step is performed according to the rules used in the case of a nonproduction unit.

This observation means that in all the areas common to both production and nonproduction units, the accounting methods used for the latter are also valid for the former. However, due to the special operations performed by the production units, that is, the production of physical goods, some extensions of the accounting procedures used with the nonproduction units are needed. These extensions will be described below.

3.2 The Balance Statement of a Production Unit

The first impact of the production process is on the balance statement. To satisfy production needs, an economic unit is likely to maintain inventories of raw materials. Also as a result of the production process, inventories of goods in process and of finished goods are likely to be maintained. These three new types of inventories are the main differences between the balance statements of a nonproduction unit and those of a production unit.

3.3 Characteristic Transactions of a Production Unit

The production process can be summarized by the following transactions: (a) purchases of raw materials; (b) use of raw materials in stock together with labor, equipment, etc., to produce finished goods; and (c) transfer of these goods from the inventory of goods in process to that of finished goods. Each of these transactions is recorded with the proper adaptation of the debit and credit rules presented in Chapter 2. The examples in Chapter 3 are described here. (The transactions are recorded in Table 3–1.)

1. Purchases of raw materials. For example, Firm A buys $100 of raw materials paid in cash.
2. Raw materials, plus wages and other production expenditures, are used in the process. For example, $20 is paid in cash for wages and $50 of raw material is used in the production process.

Observe that several payments of wages and other costs can be accumulated as work in process over the production period. It should also be observed that only costs directly related to the manufacturing process (called direct costs) are to be debited as work in process. The expenditures that do not affect production directly, such as administration costs (called indirect costs), are debited to the appropriate net worth account and balanced with the asset used to pay the expenditure, or the liability generated with the transaction.

Once the production process is finished, the goods are transferred to the inventory of finished goods. For example, the work in process is completed and a known number of finished items; say, 35, is transferred to the inventory of finished goods.

It should be observed that the record of the transfer from the inventory of work in process to the inventory of finished goods gives the cost of the goods transferred. With the information of the number of units transferred, it is possible to specify their unit cost. In the example given, the unit cost is equal to $2.

In this example, it is assumed that a batch of raw materials entered the production process and nothing else was processed until that batch was finished. In practice, of course, the production process is continuous, with raw materials continuously entering and finished goods continuously coming out. For this reason, together with the fact that the costs of raw materials, salaries, etc., are constantly changing, the estimation in practice of the unit cost of the finished goods is much more difficult. The details of this problem will not be discussed here.

The goods produced are then sold somewhat independently from the production process. These transactions are recorded, as are the sales of a nonproduction unit, in two parts. The first part records the sale itself, that is, the amount of the sale and the form in which payment is received. The second part records the reduction in the inventory of finished goods and, as a result, of the net worth of the production unit. For example, 15 units produced for $30 are sold for $80 in cash.

Table 3–1
Example for Chapter 3: Example of Transactions in Production Process

	Tangible Assets		Financial Assets		Liabilities		Net Worth	
	Debit Uses +	Credit Sources −	Debit Uses +	Credit Sources −	Debit Uses −	Credit Sources +	Debit Uses −	Credit Sources +
1. Inventory Raw Materials	100							
Cash				100				
2. Work in Process	70							
Cash Paid for Wages				20				
Inventory Raw Materials		50						
3. Inventory Finished Goods	70							
Work in Process		70						
4. Sales								80
Cash			80					
Inventory Finished Goods		30						
Cost of Goods Sold							30	

The transactions just presented as examples are recorded in Table 3–1. It should be observed that only direct costs are included. In actual accounts, however, indirect costs would usually appear.

The transactions statement in Table 3–2 is obtained from the transactions in Table 3–1.

In general, the transactions statement of a production unit takes the form of equation (2.3). In particularly simple cases, it can be presented as

$$\Delta A + \Delta T = \Delta B + S - C \tag{3.1}$$

where ΔN has been replaced with the value of sales (S) minus cost of goods sold (C).

In the part of the transactions statement of a production unit dealing with reduction of inventories of finished goods and cost of goods sold, the problem of how the expenditures made during the production process actually influence the net worth of the firm when the produced goods are sold is not discussed. A link must be built between the record of the transactions of the production process and that of the reduction of net worth caused by the sale of goods, that is, between the production process and the cost of goods sold. The following method is used for this purpose.

First, the production process is summarized in the equation:

raw materials used between t and $t + 1$

+ direct or production wages paid between
  t and $t + 1$

+ depreciation between t and $t + 1$

+ other expenditures in production between
  t and $t + 1$

is equal to $\tag{3.2}$

finished goods produced between t and $t + 1$

+ Net additions to inventory of work in
  process between t and $t + 1$

Next, each of the elements of this equation is analyzed in detail. The following identity is used for raw materials:

inventory of raw materials at date t

+ purchases of raw materials between dates
  t and $t + 1$

is equal to $\tag{3.3}$

inventory of raw materials at date $t + 1$

+ raw materials used between t and $t + 1$

Table 3–2
Example for Chapter 3: Transactions Statement

	Debit	Credit
Inventory of Raw Materials	100	50
Inventory of Work in Process	70	70
Inventory of Finished Goods	70	30
Cash	80	120
Net Worth		
Sales		80
Cost of Goods Sold	30	
Total	350	350

Similarly, the following identity can be written with respect to finished goods:

inventory of finished goods at date t

+ finished goods produced between t and $t + 1$

$$\text{is equal to} \qquad\qquad (3.4)$$

inventory of finished goods at date $t + 1$
+ cost of goods sold between t and $t + 1$

Finally, two identities can be stated dealing with work in process:

inventory of work in process at date t

+ gross additions to inventory of work in process
between t and $t + 1$

$$\text{is equal to} \qquad\qquad (3.5)$$

inventory of work in process at date $t + 1$

+ finished goods produced between t and $t + 1$

The second identity is:

net additions to inventory of work in process
between t and $t + 1$

$$\text{is equal to} \qquad\qquad (3.6)$$

gross additions to inventory of work in process
between t and $t + 1$

− finished goods produced between t and $t + 1$

To obtain the expression for the cost of goods sold in Table 3–3, the identities in equations (3.3) to (3.6) are replaced in the identity in equation

Table 3–3
Equation Relating Cost of Goods Sold with Production Process Accounting

Cost of Goods Sold =

Inventory of finished goods date t
+ Inventory of work in process date t
+ Inventory of raw materials date t
+ Raw materials purchased between t and $t + 1$
+ Direct wages paid between t and $t + 1$
+ Depreciation between t and $t + 1$
+ Other production expenditures between t and $t + 1$
− Inventory of finished goods at date $t + 1$
− Inventory of work in process at date $t + 1$
− Inventory of raw materials at date $t + 1$

Table 3–4
Cost of Goods Sold for Transactions in Table 3–1

Cost of Goods Sold =	
Inventory of finished goods Jan. 1	0
Inventory of work in process Jan. 1	0
Inventory of raw materials Jan. 1	0
Raw materials purchased Jan. 1–Dec. 30	100
− Inventory of raw materials Dec. 30	−50
Wages paid to production workers Jan. 1–Dec. 30	20
Depreciation Jan. 1–Dec. 30	0
Other production expenditures Jan. 1–Dec. 30	0
− Inventory of work in process Dec. 30	0
− Inventory of finished goods Dec. 30	−40
Cost of goods sold	30

(3.2) and cost of goods sold is left on one side of the expression. The expression in Table 3–3 is the link between the reduction of net worth due to a sale, that is, cost of goods sold, and the production process.

In the equation in Table 3–3 it is assumed that the values of the inventories at date $t + 1$ are known. The method to obtain these values is explained here. A first possibility is simply to add to the initial value of an inventory the value of all the goods added to it, and to subtract the value of all the goods taken from it. This is in essence what equations (3.2) to (3.6) do. Another possibility is physically to count and measure the goods in the inventories. In general, both procedures are used to test the compliability of the results obtained with them.

Table 3–5
Transactions Statement with Detailed Composition of Cost of Goods Sold

	Debit	Credit
Inventory of raw materials	100	50
Inventory of work in process	70	70
Inventory of finished goods	70	30
Cash	80	120
Net worth		
Sales		80
Cost of goods sold		
Inventory of finished goods Jan. 1	0	
Inventory of work in process Jan. 1	0	
Inventory of raw material Jan. 1	0	
Raw materials purchased Jan. 1–Dec. 30	100	
Inventory of raw materials Dec. 30		50
Direct wages Jan. 1–Dec. 30	20	
Depreciation	0	
Other production expenditures	0	
Inventory of work in process Dec. 30		0
Inventory of finished goods		40
Total	440	440

In Table 3–4, the cost of goods sold is computed from the transactions in Table 3–1.

With the equation in Table 3–3, the detailed composition of the cost of goods sold can be integrated with the transactions statement of the production units. Equation (3.1), in the particularly simple case in which initial and final inventory and indirect costs are zero, becomes

$$\Delta A = \Delta B + S - (wL + iB + rA + T) \qquad (3.7)$$

where w = wage rate, L = number of man hours, i = interest rate, r = depreciation rate, T = value of raw materials produced during the accounting period. When initial and final inventories do not have equal values, their difference should appear in equation (3.7).

Similarly, the transactions statement in Table 3–2 becomes that of Table 3–5.

3.4 The Income Statement

The income statement for a production unit is obtained by means of the same procedure used in the case of a nonproduction unit. For this reason, no additional explanation will be presented here.

3.5 The Accounting Process

As observed in Section 3.1, the process of going from the initial to the final balance of a production unit is basically identical to that used in the case of a nonproduction unit. The only addition to the process described in Chapter 2 is in the method of expressing the cost of goods sold in terms of the production process accounts, and then using this expression in the transactions statement.

References

Enthoven, A. J. H., *Accounting and Economic Development Policy* (Amsterdam: North Holland/American Elsevier, 1973).

Mathews, R., *Accounting for Economists* (Chapters 5, 18 and 19) (London: Angus and Robertson, 1969).

Powelson, J., *Economic Accounting* (Chapter 12) (New York: McGraw-Hill, 1955).

4

The Accounting System of the Household Sector

4.1 Purpose of This Chapter

In this chapter the principles of accounting presented in Chapter 2 are applied to a simplified set of household transactions that constitute the example for Chapter 4. There are three reasons for doing this. The first is to familiarize the reader with the main assets and liabilities of the household sector and the principal transactions it performs. The second is to show that the principles of accounting presented in Chapter 2 apply without any modification to the household sector. The description of the initial assets and liabilities of the household in the example for this chapter, as well as the description of the transactions it performs, will be used as the basis for constructing a table equivalent to Table 2–6. The final reason is that this detailed presentation of the accounts of the example for this chapter will be a part of the basic information used in constructing the examples of the macro-accounting statements.

The presentation of the actual content of assets, liabilities, and transactions of the household sector will be reinforced with the discussion in this chapter of the actual accounts compiled for households in the United States. The actual data for these sectoral accounts are not included here. They appear only as part of the macro-accounting statements.

4.2 The Balance Equation for Households

The balance equation for the nonfarm household sector of the American economy appears in Chapter 9, Table 9–1, columns (2) and (3). Some of the characteristics of this table will be explained here.

The values of tangible and financial assets appear in the debit column of households, that is, column (2). The values of liabilities and net worth appear on the credit side (column 3).

Two characteristics of the households' tangible assets can be observed: (a) housing constitutes a large percentage of the tangible assets of households, and (b) the sector does not accumulate inventories.

The only financial asset that demands explanation is insurance reserves. From the point of view of an isolated household, the payment of an insurance premium can be considered as an expenditure. It is the price

31

paid to maintain a conditional asset. Eventually, the household will receive the payment of the insurance claim, and this would increase its net worth. However, the "expenditure" in insurance does not appear as an asset. It will simply appear as a reduction of net worth in the transaction equation of the households.

When the point of view of all the households considered together is adopted, a different situation arises. This change is a result of the characteristics peculiar to insurance. These characteristics are explained here with reference to life insurance. The costs of the insurance companies such as salaries, will not be considered here. This has no effect on the explanation, because the payments of insurance companies for salaries and other costs do not differ from those of any other type of company.

In life insurance a large group of persons is considered, and by means of actuarial techniques an estimate is obtained of the average number of years the persons in the group will live. For instance, if the group has 1000 members and if 500 of them live 5 years and 500 live 25 years, the average number of years of life is 15. This average is called the expected life of a member of the group.

Next, assume that all members of the group want to receive, when they die, a fixed amount of money, say, $10,000. In order to determine the premiums they should pay, the insurance company assumes that all the members of the group will die when they complete their expected life. No one dies any sooner or any later. With such assumptions, the premium should be equal to the annuity required to accumulate, in the number of years equal to the expected life, the amount that should be paid to all the insured. In other words, each person insured is saving a certain amount per year to accumulate a capital in a fixed number of years. The total amount saved each year would be the annual increment of the reserve of the insurance company. Taken in this way, it is clear that such a reserve is an asset for the policy holders. It is simply the accumulation of their savings.

In actual practice, not all persons insured die simultaneously on the date when the period of their life expectancy ends. The number of deaths is more or less evenly distributed in time. At the beginning, most of the insured persons are alive and pay their premiums. For this reason, the total of premiums received by the insurance company at the beginning of the period is larger than the claims it has to pay. The difference between the receipts of the company and the claims on it is the reserve of the company. Again, this reserve is savings for the policy holders.

The liabilities of the households sector presents another important characteristic: their total is extremely low when compared with total assets. This fact will be more evident when the other economic sectors are compared. It is mentioned here because it characterizes the household sector. Households typically are a sector that supplies savings. It will be seen later that these savings go through the financial institutions to the firms producing goods and services.

The composition of the liabilities of households should also be noted. The heavy emphasis on mortgage can be easily understood.

Later in this chapter, in Table 4–4, columns (2) and (3), the balance statement for the example for Chapter 4 is presented. This statement has characteristics similar to those observed for the household sector of the American economy.

4.3 Transactions for Households

4.3.1 Recording of the Transactions

The example for Chapter 4 deals with the transactions of the household sector. The principles presented in Section 2.4.2 are used to record the following transactions in Table 4–1. The numbers in parentheses indicate the other sectors participating in a transaction, and the transaction in which the operation is recorded. The following notation is used: 1, Households; 2, Industry; 3, Banks; 4, Government; 5, Rest of the World.

1. Households (Hh) receive the following payments from industry (Ind):
   (a) $22.40 for rents: $18 by check and $4.40 in cash (TR 2, 4, a; TR 3, 11, a);
   (b) $307.40 for direct wages: $250 by check and $57.40 in cash (TR 2, 4, b; TR 2, 11, b);
   (c) $105.50 for indirect wages: $90 by check and $15.50 in cash (TR 2, 4, c; TR 3, 11, c);
   (d) $29.30 in interest: $25 by check and $4.30 in cash (TR 2, 7, a; TR 3, 11, d);
   (e) $23.20 as profits received by check (TR 2, 8, a; TR 3, 11, e).

2. Households purchase from homeland (HL) Ind:
   (a) Consumption goods worth $481.20: $400 paid by check, $50 in cash, $31.20 credit (TR 2, 10, c; TR 3, 12, a);
   (b) Capital goods worth $21.10: $15 paid by check, $3 in cash, $3.10 credit (TR 2, 10, d; TR 3, 12, b).

3. Households purchase from Rest of the World (RW) Ind:
   (a) Consumption goods worth $4.80: $4 paid by check, $0.80 credit (TR 3, 15, d; TR 5, 5, a);

Table 4–1
Example for Chapter 4: Record of Household Transactions

Concept	Tangible Assets		Financial Assets		Liabilities		Net Worth	
	+Debit	−Credit	+Debit	−Credit	−Debit	+Credit	−Debit	+Credit
1a. Rents Ind								22.4
Deposits Ind			18.0					
Cash Ind			4.4					
1b. Direct Wages Ind								307.4
Deposits Ind			250.0					
Cash Ind			57.4					
1c. Indirect Wages Ind								105.5
Deposits Ind			90.0					
Cash Ind			15.5					
1d. Interest Ind								29.3
Deposits Ind			25.0					
Cash Ind			4.3					
1e. Profits Ind								23.2
Deposits Ind			23.2					
2a. Consumption Ind							481.2	
Deposits Ind				400				
Cash Ind				50				
Accounts Payable Ind						31.2		
2b. Capital	21.1							
Deposits Ind				15.0				
Cash Ind				3.0				
Accounts Payable Ind						3.1		
3a. Consumption RW							4.8	
Deposits RW				4.0				
Accounts Payable RW						0.8		

No.	Account		
3b.	Capital RW	1.7	
	Deposits RW		1.7
4a.	Services Bk	10.1	
	Deposits Bk		7.0
	Cash Bk		2.0
	Accounts Payable Bk		1.1
4b.	Services RW Bk	1.1	
	Deposits RW		1.1
5.	Capital Consumption	8.7	
	Depreciation		8.7
6.	Tax Gov	75.2	
	Deposits Gov		35.0
	Cash Gov		40.2
7a.	Interests Bk	12.4	
	Deposits Bk		9.0
	Cash Bk		3.4
7b.	Interest Gov	9.9	
	Deposits Gov		8.0
	Cash Gov		1.9
8a.	Wages Bk	14.6	
	Deposits Bk		10.0
	Cash Bk		4.6
8b.	Wages Gov	117.8	
	Deposits Gov		105.0
	Cash Gov		12.8
8c.	Wages RW	2.1	
	Deposits RW		2.1
9.	Profits Bk	1.4	
	Deposits Bk		1.4
10.	Cash Withdraw	20.0	
	Deposits Withdraw		20.0

Table 4–1 (cont.)

Concept	Tangible Assets +Debit	Tangible Assets −Credit	Financial Assets +Debit	Financial Assets −Credit	Liabilities −Debit	Liabilities +Credit	Net Worth −Debit	Net Worth +Credit
11a. Bonds Gov			15.0					
Deposits Gov				15.0				
11b. Bonds Bk			5.0					
Deposits Bks				5.0				
11c. Securities Ind			40.0					
Deposits Ind				25.0				
Cash Ind				15.0				
11d. Securities RW			5.0					
Deposits Bks				5.0				
11e. Securities RW			2.0					
Deposits RW				2.0				
11f. Shares Ind			15.0					
Deposits Ind				13.0				
Cash Ind				2.0				
11g. Shares Bk			3.0					
Deposits Bk				3.0				
12. Cash Deposits			25.0					
Deposits				25.0				
13. Securities Ind			10.0					
Deposits Ind				10.0				
14. Gov Ind Bk			5.0					
Deposits Bk				5.0				
Total	22.8	8.7	791.0	704.0	—	36.2	581.1	646.0

    (b) Capital goods worth $1.70: paid by check (TR 3, 15, e; TR 5, 5, b).

4. Households pay for services provided to:

    (a) HL banks (Bk) $10.10: $7 reducing Hh deposit account, $2 cash, $1.10 credit (TR 3, 3);

    (b) RW Bk $1.10: by check (TR 3, 15, f; TR 5, 5, c).

5. Capital goods owned by Hh depreciate by $8.70.

6. Households pay taxes of $75.20: $35 by check, $40.20 cash (TR 3, 14, a; TR 4, 1, a).

7. Households receive interest payments:

    (a) From Bk for $12.40: $9 paid increasing Hh deposit account, $3.40 in cash (TR 3, 4, a);

    (b) From government (Gov) for $9.90: $8 paid by check, $1.90 in cash (TR 3,11, f; TR 4, 3, a).

8. Households receive wages:

    (a) From Bk for $14.60: $10 paid increasing Hh deposit account, $4.60 in cash (TR 3, 4, b);

    (b) From Gov for $117.80: $105 paid by check, $12.80 cash (TR 3, 11, g, TR 4, 3, b);

    (c) From RW for $2.10: paid by check (TR 3, 11, h; TR 5, 7).

9. Households receive $1.40 profits from Bk: payment increasing Hh deposit account (TR 3, 6).

10. Houeholds withdraw $20 from their deposit account (TR 3, 16).

11. Households buy:

    (a) Government bonds from Gov for $15: paid by check (TR 3, 14, d; TR 4, 6);

    (b) Government bonds from Bk for $5: paid with a reduction of Hh deposit account (TR 3, 17);

    (c) Securities from Ind for $40: $25 paid by check, $15 in cash (TR 2, 14; TR 3, 12, e);

    (d) Securities from Bk for $5: paid reducing Hh deposit account (TR 3, 18);

    (e) Securities from RW for $2: paid by check (TR 3, 15, j; TR 5, 13);

    (f) Shares from Ind for $15: $13 paid by check, $2 in cash (TR 2, 15; TR 3, 12, f);

    (g) Shares from Bk for $3: paid reducing Hh deposit account (TR 3, 19).

12. Households deposit $25 in their deposit account (TR 3, 20).

Table 4–2
Example for Chapter 4: Preparation of the Detailed Transactions Statement from Records in Table 4–1[a]

Transactions		Debit	Credit
Tangible Assets, Purchases of Capital, and Depreciation			
Hh	*Ind*		
2b	10d	21.1	
Hh	*Bk*		
Hh	*Hh*		
5 Capital Consumption			8.7
Depreciation		8.7	
Hh	*RW*		
3b		1.7	
Cash			
Hh	*Ind*		
1a	4a	4.4	
1b	4b	57.4	
1c	4c	15.5	
1d	7a	4.3	
2a	10c		50.0
2b	10d		3.0
11c	14		15.0
11f	15		2.0
Total		81.6	70.0
Hh	*Gov*		
6	1a		40.2
7b	3a	1.9	
8b	3b	12.8	
Total		14.7	40.2
Hh	*Bk*		
4a	3		2.0
7a	7a	3.4	
8a	4b	4.6	
10	16	20.0	
12	20		25.0
Total		28.0	27.0
Hh	*RW*		
Deposits			
Hh	*Ind*		
1a	4a	18.0	
1b	4b	250.0	
1c	4c	90.0	
1d	7a	25.0	

[a]References to transaction numbers in sectors other than households (Hh) are derived from the following tables (presented later in this book): Ind, Table 5–1; Bk, Table 6–5; Gov, Table 7–1; RW, Table 8–1.

Table 4–2 (cont.)

Transactions		Debit	Credit
1e	8a	23.2	
2a	10c		400.0
2b	10d		15.0
11c	14		25.0
11f	15		13.0
13	16	10.0	
Total		416.2	453.0
Hh	Gov		
6	1a		35.0
7b	3a	8.0	
8b	3b	105.0	
11a	6		15.0
Total		113.0	50.0
Hh	Bk		
4a	3		7.0
7a	4a	9.0	
8a	4b	10.0	
9	6	1.4	
10	16		20.0
11b	17		5.0
11d	18		5.0
11g	19		3.0
12	20	25.0	
14	21	5.0	
Total		50.4	40.0
Hh	RW		
3a	5a		4.0
3b	5b		1.7
4b	5c		1.1
8c	7	2.1	
11e	13		2.0
Total		2.1	8.8

Financial Assets and Liabilities

		Debit	Credit
Hh	Ind		
2a Accounts Payable	10c		31.2
2b Accounts Payable	10d		3.1
11c Securities	14	40.0	
11f Shares	15	15.0	
12 Securities	16		10.0
Total		55.0	44.3
Hh	Gov		
11a Bonds	6	15.0	
Hh	Bk		
4a Accounts Payable	3		1.1
11b Bonds Bk	17	5.0	
11d Securities Bk	18	5.0	
11g Shares	19	3.0	
14 Bonds Bk	21		5.0
Total		13.0	6.1

Table 4–2 (cont.)

Transactions		Debit	Credit
	Wages		
Hh	*Ind*		
1b	4b		307.4
1c	4c		105.5
Total			412.9
Hh	*Gov*		
8b	3b		117.8
Hh	*Bk*		
8a	4b		14.6
Hh	*RW*		
8c	7		2.1
	Rents, Profits and Interest		
Hh	*Ind*		
1a Rents			22.4
1d Interest			29.3
1e Profits			23.2
Hh	*Bk*		
7a Interest			12.4
9 Profits			1.4
Hh	*Gov*		
7b Interest			9.9
Hh	*RW*		
	Consumption of Goods and Services		
Hh	*Ind*		
2a	10c	481.2	
Hh	*Gov*		
Hh	*Bk*		
4a	3	10.1	
Hh	*RW*		
3a	5a	4.8	
4b	5c	1.1	

13. Households receive payment of $10 from Ind (i.e., households sell to Ind securities issued by Ind: payment by check (TR 2, 16; TR 3, 11, i).
14. Banks buy $5 of government bonds from Hh: payment increasing Hh deposit account (TR 3, 21).

4.3.2 The Transactions Statement for Households

Once the transactions are recorded, it is possible to proceed with the preparation of the transactions statement for households.

Table 4–3
Example for Chapter 4: Detailed Transactions Statement for Households

	Debit	*Credit*
Tangible Assets		
Purchase Capital Goods		
Ind	21.1	
RW	1.7	
Capital Consumption		8.7
Financial Assets and Liabilities		
Cash		
Ind	81.6	70.0
Bk	28.0	27.0
Gov	14.7	40.2
Deposits		
Ind	416.2	453.0
Bk	50.4	40.0
Gov	113.0	50.0
RW	2.1	8.8
Other		
Ind	55.0	44.3
Bk	13.0	6.1
Gov	15.0	—
RW	2.0	0.8
Total Assets & Liabilities	813.8	748.9
Net Worth		
Wages		
Ind		412.9
Bk		14.6
Gov		117.8
RW		2.1
Rents		
Ind		22.4
Interests		
Ind		29.3
Bk		12.4
Gov		9.9
Profits		
Ind		23.2
Bk		1.4
Consumption		
Ind	481.2	
Bk	10.1	
RW	5.9	
Taxes	75.2	
Depreciation	8.7	
Total Net Worth	581.1	646.0
Total	1,394.9	1,394.9

Table 4–4

Example for Chapter 4: Summary of the Accounting Process for the Household Sector

Accounts (1)	Initial Balance Debit (2)	Credit (3)	Transactions Statement Debit (4)	Credit (5)	Income Statement Debit (6)	Credit (7)	Final Balance Debit (8)	Credit (9)
Tangible Assets								
Consumer Durables	43.2						43.2	
Land/Structures	107.1		22.8	8.7			121.2	
Financial Assets								
Cash	42.4		124.3	137.2			29.5	
Deposits	95.6		581.7	551.8			125.5	
Accounts Receivable	82.5						82.5	
Securities	35.1		47.0	10.0			72.1	
Shares	2315.9		18.0				2333.9	
Gov Bonds	95.8		20.0	5.0			110.8	
Liabilities								
Accounts Payable		50.3		36.2				86.5
Net Worth		2767.3						2767.3
Wages				547.4		547.4		
Rents				22.4		22.4		
Interests				51.6		51.6		
Profits				24.6		24.6		
Consumption			497.2		497.2			
Taxes			75.2		75.2			
Depreciation			8.7		8.7			
Savings					64.9			64.9
Total	2817.6	2817.6	1394.9	1394.9	646.0	646.0	2918.7	2918.7

In order to prepare the detailed national transactions table (see Chapter 10, Table 10–1), it is necessary to modify the procedure described in Chapter 2 for the preparation of the transactions statement. In the present case, all the debits should be added to the debits and all the credits to the credits affecting one account. The same should be done for all transactions within the same sector. As a result of this, for example, transactions affecting cash will be classified as transactions with other households, with industry, banking, government, and rest of the world. The same is true for all the other accounts.

The procedure to be used for the preparation of the detailed transaction statement appears in Table 4–2.

The detailed transactions statement for households in Table 4–3 is obtained using the totals by account and by sector obtained in Table 4–2.

The transactions statement for the household sector of the United States in 1966 appears in Chapter 10, Table 10–2, columns (2) and (3). As already observed, no data are available for the preparation of a detailed statement. It should be observed that columns (2) and (3) of Table 10–2 are equivalent to columns (4) and (5) of Table 2–6.

4.4 The Income Statement for Households

The income statement for households is obtained by following the rules presented in Chapters 2 and 3. It can be read from the net worth section of the transactions statement in Table 4–3 and from the net worth part of Table 10–2 for the household sector of the United States. The difference between debits and credits to net worth, that is, the net income for households, is presented in the bottom part of Table 10–2.

4.5 Summary of the Accounting Process for Households

The summary of the accounting process for households in the example for this chapter is presented in Table 4–4. As in the case of Table 2–6, it includes the initial balance, the transactions during the period, the income statement, and the final balance. The columns in this table can be considered as a detailed expression of equations (2.2) and (2.3).

Reference

Powelson, J. *Economic Accounting* (Chapter 2) (New York: McGraw Hill, 1955).

5

The Accounting System of the Industrial Sector

5.1 Purpose of This Chapter

The industrial sector of an economy includes several types of agricultural, manufacturing, and service enterprises.

This chapter presents an additional application of the principles of micro-accounting explained in Chapters 2 and 3, and it should familiarize the reader with the principal assets and liabilities as well as the transactions of the industrial units.

In the example for this chapter only one industry is considered. This is enough, though barely so, to provide the information needed to construct a set of macro-accounts. However, in the exercise, three industrial sectors are considered: agriculture, manufacturing, and services. The reader should keep these three types of units separate. This will be useful in the construction of input/output tables.

5.2 Balance Equation for the Industrial Sector

The industrial sector of the American economy is composed of nonfinancial corporate enterprises, nonfinancial noncorporate enterprises, and agriculture. (The characteristics of financial enterprises are discussed in Chapter 6.) The balance for this consolidated sector in 1966 appears in Chapter 9, Table 9–1.

The main similarities and differences that appear, when columns (2) and (3) for households and columns (4) and (5) for industry in Table 9–1 are compared, are the following:

1. Tangible assets have a higher percentage for industry than for households.
2. This larger percentage is due to the importance of producer durables and inventories for industry, items that almost never appear in households.
3. The percentage of cash and demand deposits as compared with total financial assets is higher for industry than for households. This means that the liquidity of industry is higher.

4. The higher liquidity of industry is related to its higher percentage of liabilities, in particular of the short-term variety. Where longer term liabilities (for example, mortgages) are considered, households have a higher percentage.

5. The net worth of industry is lower in percentage than that of households, as a result of industry's higher liabilities.

The initial balance statement for the industrial sector in the example for this chapters appears later in Table 5–5, columns (2) and (3).

5.3 Transactions for Industry

5.3.1 Recording of the Transactions

The transactions performed by an industry during an accounting period are presented in the example for Chapter 5:

1. Industry purchases raw materials from RW industry for $15.40, $10 paid by check, $5.40 in credit (TR 3, 5, a; TR 5, 1).

2. Industry uses from its inventories of raw materials:

   (a) In its production process, goods valued at $764.80

   (b) From RW, goods valued at $15.40

3. The capital goods of the manufacturing sector depreciate by $53.70.

4. The manufacturing sector pays to Hh.

   (a) Rents for building used in the production process of $22.40: $18 paid by check, $4.40 in cash (TR 1, 1; TR 3, 11, a);

   (b) Direct wages of $307.40: $250 paid by check, $57.40 in cash (TR 1, 1, b; TR 3, 11, b);

   (c) Indirect wages of $105.50: $90 paid by check, $15.50 in cash (TR 1, 1, c; TR 3, 11, c).

5. Industry transfers 100 units of finished goods valued at $1150 from the production process to the inventory of finished goods

6. Industry pays for services provided, $34.80 to HL Bk: $25 paid by check, $9.80 in cash (TR 3, 1)

7. Industry pays:

   (a) To Hh $29.30 in interest: $25 paid by check, $4.30 in cash (TR 1, 1, d; TR 3, 11, d);

   (b) To RW households, $1.50 in interest: paid by check (TR 3, 15, b; TR 5, 2).

8. Industry pays dividends to:

   (a) To Hh, $23.20: paid by check (TR 1, 1, e; TR 3, 11, e);
   (b) To RW, $2.10: paid by check (TR 3, 15, c; TR 5, 3).

9. Industry pays $91.60 in taxes to Gov: $85.00 by check, $6.60 in cash (TR 3, 14, b; TR 4, 1, b).

10. Industry sells goods:

    (a) To Bk, raw materials for $6: $4 increasing Ind deposits, the rest cash. Cost of goods sold, $2.93 (TR 3, 2, a);
    (b) To Bk, capital goods for $5.90: paid increasing Ind deposit account. Cost of goods sold, $2.88 (TR 3, 2, b);
    (c) To Hh, consumption goods for $481.20: $400 paid by check, $50 in cash, $31.20 credit. Cost of goods sold, $235 (TR 1, 2, a; TR 3, 12, a);
    (d) To Hh, capital goods for $21.10: $15 paid by check, $3.00 in cash, $3.10 credit. Cost of goods sold, $10.30 (TR 1, 2, b; TR 3, 12, b);
    (e) To Gov for $74.50: $60 paid by check, $10 in cash, $4.50 credit. Cost of goods sold, $36.39 (TR 3, 12, c; TR 4, 2);
    (f) To RW for $38.50: $35 paid by check, $3.50 in credit. Cost of goods sold, $18.80 (TR 3, 12, d; TR 5, 4).

11. Industry uses its own production:

    (a) To refill inventories of raw materials. Goods used have a cost of $764.80;
    (b) As capital goods. Goods used have a value of $77.60. These transactions are sale of Ind to itself.

12. Industry purchases from RW capital goods for $3.20: $2.50 paid by check, $0.70 credit (TR 3, 15, g; TR 5, 6, a).

13. Industry uses RW Bk services for $4.70: paid by check (TR 3, 15, i; TR 5, 12).

14. Industry sells securities (promises to pay) to Hh for $40: $25 paid by check, $15 in cash (TR 1, 11, c; TR 3, 12, e).

15. Industry sells shares to Hh for $15: $13 paid by check, $2 in cash (TR 1, 11, f; TR 3, 12, f).

16. Industry pays to Hh $10 (that is, industry buys from households securities issued by industry): paid by check (TR 1, 13; TR 3, 11, i).

17. Industry withdraws $5 from its deposits account (TR 3, 22).

18. Industry sells shares for $8 to RW: paid by check (TR 3, 12, g; TR 5, 14).

19. Industry deposits $10 in its deposit account (TR 3, 23).

Table 5–1
Example for Chapter 5: Recording of Industry's Transactions

Concept	Tangible Assets		Financial Assets		Liabilities		Net Worth	
	+Debit	−Credit	+Debit	−Credit	−Debit	+Credit	−Debit	+Credit
1. Inventory Raw Materials RW	15.4							
Deposits RW				10.0				
Accounts Payable RW						5.4		
2a. Inventory Raw Materials Ind	764.8							
Inventory W Proc. Ind		764.8						
2b. Inventory Raw Materials RW		15.4						
Inventory Work in Process	15.4							
3. Capital Cons.		53.7						
Inventory Work in Process	53.7							
4a. Rents Hh Work in Process	22.4							
Deposits Hh				18.0				
Cash Hh				4.4				
4b. Wages Work in Process	307.4							
Deposits Hh				250.0				
Cash Hh				57.4				
4c. Wages							105.5	
Deposits Hh				90.0				
Cash Hh				15.5				
5. Inventory Work in Process		1150.0						
Inventory Finished Goods	1150.0							
6. Services Bk							34.8	
Deposits Bk				25.0				
Cash Bk				9.8				

	Account				
7a.	Interest Hh		29.3		
	Deposits Hh			25.0	
	Cash Hh			4.3	
7b.	Interest Hh RW		1.5		
	Deposits RW			1.5	
8a.	Profits Hh		23.2		
	Deposits Hh			23.2	
8b.	Profits Hh RW		2.1		
	Deposits Hh RW			2.1	
9.	Tax Gov		91.6		
	Deposits Gov			85.0	
	Cash Gov			6.6	
10a.	Sales to Bk	6.0			
	Deposits Bk			4.0	
	Cash Bk			2.0	
	Cost of Goods		2.93		
	Inv. Finished				2.93
10b.	Sales to Bk	5.9			
	Deposits Bk			5.9	
	Cost of Goods		2.88		
	Inventory Finished				2.88
10c.	Sales to Hh	481.2			
	Deposits Hh			400.0	
	Cash Hh			50.0	
	Accounts Receivable Hh			31.2	
	Cost of Goods		235.0		
	Inventory Finished				235.0
10d.	Sales to Hh	21.1			
	Deposits Hh			15.0	
	Cash Hh			3.0	
	Accounts Receivable Hh			3.1	
	Cost of Goods		10.30		
	Inventory Finished				10.30

Table 5–1 (cont.)

Concept	Tangible Assets +Debit	Tangible Assets −Credit	Financial Assets +Debit	Financial Assets −Credit	Liabilities −Debit	Liabilities +Credit	Net Worth −Debit	Net Worth +Credit
10e. Sales to Gov								74.5
Deposits Gov			60.0					
Cash Gov			10.0					
Accounts Receivable Gov			4.5					
Cost of Goods							36.39	
Inventory Finished		36.39						
10f. Sales to RW								38.5
Deposits RW			35.0					
Accounts Receivable RW			3.5					
Cost of Goods							18.80	
Inv. Finished		18.80						
11a. Sales to Ind								764.8
Inventory Raw Materials	764.8							
Cost of Goods							764.8	
Inventory Finished		764.8						
11b. Sales to Ind								77.6
Capital	77.6							
Cost of Goods							77.6	
Inventory Finished		77.6						
12. Capital RW	3.2							
Deposits RW				2.5				
Accounts Payable RW						0.7		
13. Services RW Bk							4.7	
Dep. RW				4.7				
14. Securities to Hh						40.0		
Deposits Hh			25.0					
Cash Hh			15.0					

15. Shares to Hh			15.0					
Deposits Hh						13.0		
Cash Hh						2.0		
16. Securities for Hh					10.0			
Deposits Hh				10.0				
17. Cash Bk Deposits					5.0			
Deposits						5.0		
18. Shares to RW			8.0					
Deposits RW						8.0		
19. Cash to Deposits					10.0			
Deposits						10.0		
20. Accounts Payable Bk			5.0					
Deposits Bk						5.0		
Total	1469.6	1141.4	73.4	10.0	660.7	710.2	3132.60	3174.7

Table 5–2
Example for Chapter 5: Preparation of Detailed Transactions Statement for Industry from Records in Table 5–1

Transactions		Debit	Credit
	Cash		
Ind	*Hh*		
4a	1a		4.4
4b	1b		57.4
4c	1c		15.5
7a	1d		4.3
10c	2a	50.0	
10d	2b	3.0	
14	11c	15.0	
15	11f	2.0	
Total		70.0	81.6
Ind	*Gov*		
9	1b		6.6
10c	2	10.0	
Total		10.0	6.6
Ind	*Bk*		
6	1		9.8
10a	2a	2.0	
17	22	5.0	
19	23		10.0
Total		7.0	19.8
Ind	*RW*		
	Deposits		
Ind	*Hh*		
4a	1a		18.0
4b	1b		250.0
4c	1c		90.0
7a	1d		25.0
8a	1e		23.2
10c	2a	400.0	
10d	2b	15.0	
14	11c	25.0	
15	11f	13.0	
16			10.0
Total		453.0	416.2
Ind	*Gov*		
9	1b		85.0
10e	2	60.0	
Ind	*Bk*		
6	1		25.0
10a	2a	4.0	
10b	2b	5.9	
17	22		5.0
19	23	10.0	
20	24	5.0	
Total		24.9	30.0

Table 5–2 (cont.)

Transactions		Debit	Credit
Ind	*RW*		
1	1		10.0
7b	2		1.5
8b	3		2.1
10f	4	35.0	
12	6a		2.5
13	12		4.7
18	14	8.0	
Total		43.0	20.8

Financial Assets and Liabilities

Ind	*Hh*		
10c Accounts Receivable	2a	31.2	
10d Accounts Receivable	2b	3.1	
14 Securities	11c		40.0
15 Shares	11f		15.0
16 Securities	13	10.0	
Total		44.3	55.0
Ind	*Gov*		
10c Accounts Receivable	2	4.5	
Ind	*Bk*		
20 Accounts Payable	24		5.0
Ind	*RW*		
1 Accounts Payable	1		5.4
10f Accounts Receivable	4	3.5	
12 Accounts Payable	6a		0.7
18 Shares	14		8.0
Total		3.5	14.1

Wages

Ind	*Hh*		
4b	1b	307.4	
4c	1c	105.5	
Ind	*Gov*		
Ind	*Bk*		
Ind	*RW*		

Sales

Ind	*Hh*		
10c Consumption	2a		481.2
10d Capital	2b		21.1
Ind	*Ind*		
11a Consumption			764.8
11b Capital			77.6
Ind	*Bk*		
10a Consumption			6.0
10b Capital			5.9
Ind	*Gov*		
10e Consumption	2		74.5

Table 5–2 (cont.)

Transactions		Debit	Credit
Ind	RW		
10f			38.5
	Inventories		
Inventory of Raw Materials	HL		
2a			764.8
11a		764.8	
Inventory of Raw Materials	RW		
1		15.4	
2b			15.4
Inventory of Work in Process			
2a		764.8	
2b		15.4	
3		53.7	
4a		22.4	
4b		307.4	
5			1150.0
Total		1163.7	1150.0
Inventory of Finished Goods			
5		1150.0	
10a			2.93
10b			2.88
10c			235.00
10d			10.30
10e			36.39
10f			18.80
11a			764.80
11b			77.60
Total		1150.0	1148.70

20. Industry obtains a loan from Bk of $5. Loan increases Ind deposit account (TR 3, 24).

The procedures that should be used to record these transactions are described in Section 3.3. The results obtained by applying these principles appear in Table 5–1.

In Table 5–1 it should be observed that the transfers of industry's finished goods to its inventory of raw materials or to its stock of capital are treated as sales (TR 2, 11, a and b).

The sale of securities is simply the act of obtaining a credit; it is an increase in the liabilities of the industry compensated with debits, that is, increase in whatever assets the loan is received. The same is valid with respect to the sale of shares.

Table 5–3
Example for Chapter 5: Evaluation of the Composition of Cost of Goods Sold from Records in Table 5–1

Cost of Goods Sold	Debit	Credit
Inventory of Finished Goods date *t*	18.2	
Inventory of Work in Process date *t*	15.3	
Inventory of Raw Materials Ind HL date *t*	805.9	
Inventory of Raw Materials Ind RW date *t*		
Purchases of Raw Materials between *t* and *t* + 1		
Ind HL	764.8	
Ind RW	15.4	
Inventory of Finished Goods *t* + 1		19.5
Inventory of Work in Process *t* + 1		29.0
Inventory of Raw Materials *t* + 1		805.9
Ind HL		
Ind RW		
Direct Wages	307.4	
Rents	22.4	
Depreciation	53.7	
	2003.1	854.4
Cost of Goods Sold		1148.7

5.3.2 The Transactions Statement for Industry

As the first step in the preparation of the transactions statement, the entries in all transactions dealing with one account were added together. This is done in Table 5–2 with respect to the transactions recorded in Table 5–1. As in the case of households in Chapter 4, the entries are classified not only by account, but also by sector. This is done in order to prepare the transactions statement to be used in the detailed national transactions table in Chapter 10.

As observed in Chapter 3, an additional step dealing with the cost of goods sold is needed in the case of industrial units. The total cost of goods sold is obtained as a debit to net worth in the process described. The composition of this total in terms of the cost of the inputs used in the production process is obtained with the formula in Table 3–3. The application of this formula to the example for this chapter appears in Table 5–3.

The detailed transaction statement derived from Tables 5–2 and 5–3 is presented in Table 5–4.

Table 5–4
Example for Chapter 5: Detailed Transactions Statement for Industry Derived from Tables 5–2 and 5–3

Tangible Assets	Debit	Credit
Purchases Capital		
Ind	77.6	
RW	3.2	
Capital Consumption		53.7
Inventories Raw Material		
Ind	764.8	764.8
RW	15.4	15.4
Inventory Work in Process	1,163.7	1,150.0
Inventory of Finished Goods	1,150.0	1,148.7
Financial Assets and Liabilities		
Cash		
Hh	70.0	81.6
Bk	7.0	19.8
Gov	10.0	6.6
Deposits		
Hh	453.0	416.2
Bk	24.9	30.0
Gov	60.0	85.0
RW	43.0	20.8
Other		
Hh	44.3	55.0
Bk	—	5.0
Gov	4.5	—
RW	3.5	14.1
Total Assets & Liabilities	3,894.9	3,866.7
Net Worth		
Sales		
Hh Consumption		481.2
Hh Capital		21.1
Ind Intermediate		764.8
Ind Capital		77.6
Bk Intermediate		6.0
Bk Capital		5.9
Gov Consumption		74.5
RW		38.5

Table 5–4 (cont.)

Tangible Assets	Debit	Credit
Cost of Goods Sold		
Δ Inventory Finished Goods		1.3
Δ Inventory of Work in Process		13.7
Direct Wages	307.4	
Rents	22.4	
Depreciation	53.7	
Purchases Ind	764.8	
Purchases RW	15.4	
Indirect Wages	105.5	
Purchases Bk HL	34.8	
Interest Hh HL	29.3	
Interest Hh RW	1.5	
Profits Hh HL	23.2	
Profits Hh RW	2.1	
Tax	91.6	
Purchases Bk RW	4.7	
Total Net Worth	1,456.4	1,484.6
Total	5,351.3	5,351.3

5.4 The Income Statement for Industry

The income statement for industry is evaluated by means of the standard procedure, that is, as the difference between credits and debits to net worth. Basically it is composed of nondistributed profits.

The income statement for industry, derived from the net worth part of the statement in Table 5–4, appears in Table 5–5.

5.5 Summary of the Accounting Process for Industry

A summary of the accounting process for industry is presented in Table 5–5.

Table 5–5
Example for Chapter 5: Summary of the Accounting Process of the Industrial Sectors

Accounts (1)	Initial Balance		Transactions Statement		Income Statement		Final Balance	
	Debit (2)	Credit (3)	Debit (4)	Credit (5)	Debit (6)	Credit (7)	Debit (8)	Credit (9)
Tangible Assets								
Land/Structure	800.4						800.4	
Equipment	1,125.0		80.8	53.7			1,152.1	
Inventory Raw Materials	805.9		780.2	780.2			805.9	
Inventory Work in Process	15.3		1,163.7	1,150.0			29.0	
Inventory Finished Goods	18.2		1,150.0	1,148.7			19.5	
Financial Assets								
Cash	74.5		87.0	108.0			53.5	
Deposits	115.2		580.9	552.0			144.1	
Accounts Receivable	41.2		42.3				83.5	
Gov Bonds	15.3						15.3	
Liabilities								
Accounts Payable		11.7	10.0	11.1				22.8
Securities		213.8		40.0				243.8
Shares		2,513.5		23.0				2,536.5
Net Worth		272.0						300.2
Sales				1,469.6		1,469.6		
Change Inventories				15.0		15.0		
Wages			412.9		412.9			
Rents			22.4		22.4			
Depreciation			53.7		53.7			
Raw Materials			780.2		780.2			
Bank Services			39.5		39.5			
Interests			30.8		30.8			
Distributed Profits			25.3		25.3			
Tax			91.6		91.6			
Nondistributed profits					28.2			
Total	3,011.0	3,011.0	5,351.3	5,351.3	1,484.6	1,484.6	3,103.3	3,103.3

References

Enthoven, A.J.H., *Accounting and Economic Development Policy* (Chapter 3) (Amsterdam: North Holland/American Elsevier, 1973).

Mathews, R., *Accounting for Economists* (Chapters 5, 18 and 19) (London: Angus and Robertson, 1969).

Powelson, J., *Economic Accounting* (Chapter 12) (New York: McGraw Hill, 1955).

6

The Accounting System of the Financial Sectors

6.1 Purpose of This Chapter

The purpose of this chapter is to describe briefly the main economic units in the financial sector, namely, the monetary authorities, to be called central banks; the commercial banks; and nonbank financial institutions. The roles that these three types of economic units play in the determination of the money supply and the transfer of financial resources from one sector to another will then be studied. The balance, transactions, and income statements of these institutions will be used for this purpose.

The fact that the accounting principles presented in Chapters 2 and 3 apply without modification to financial institutions will also be emphasized.

6.2 Balance Equations for the Financial Sectors

The balance equations for the three types of financial institutions considered are presented in Table 6–1. The characteristics of these balances are a consequence of the special functions of the financial institutions in the economic processes. The value of their tangible assets is quite low. Their balances include almost exclusively financial assets and liabilities.

The assets of the central banks are basically (a) gold and other monetary metals, (b) holdings of foreign currency, (c) deposits in other national and foreign banks, and (d) government bonds, that is, certificates of the government debt. Of these assets, gold has a special characteristic. It is a financial asset only for central banks. For the mining companies producing it, it is a tangible asset. This emphasizes the fact that the classification is arbitrary.

Almost all the liabilities of the central banks are currency, such as coins and bills, and demand deposits. The central banks are the only institutions that have currency as a liability. It forms part of the assets of commercial banks and all other sectors.

The percentage of net worth of the central banks is extremely low. This is a consequence of a basic characteristic of financial intermediaries.

For the analysis to be made here of the supply of money, the balance equation of the central banks will be summarized as follows:

Table 6–1

Balance Statement, United States Financial System (1966 Data in 10⁹ Dollars)

	Monetary Authorities	Commercial Banks	Nonbank Finance	Total
1. *Tangible Assets*[a]	0.2	4.8	8.9	13.9
2. *Financial Assets*	67.3	356.9	573.5	997.7
a. Gold and Foreign Exchange[b]	14.0			14.0
b. Treasury Currency	6.2			6.2
c. U.S. Gov Securities	44.3	63.4	33.7	141.4
d. State and Local Obligations		41.0	16.7	57.7
e. Federal Reserve Float	2.5			2.5
f. Federal Reserve Loans to Domestic Banks	0.2			0.2
g. Corporate Bonds and Foreign Bonds		0.9	98.4	99.3
h. Corporate Stocks			91.7	91.7
i. Mortgages		54.0	235.3	289.3
j. Consumer Credit		38.9	34.5	73.4
k. Bank Loans NEC		112.1		112.1
l. Other Loans		5.2	25.4	30.6
m. Cash and Deposits			13.5	13.5
n. Time and Savings Deposits			0.2	0.2
o. Savings and Loan Shares			0.3	0.3
p. Security Credit		9.0	6.8	15.8
q. Trade Credit			2.9	2.9
r. Miscellaneous		7.4	14.3	21.7
s. Vault Cash		5.5		5.5
t. Reserves		19.8		19.8
3. *Liabilities*	67.3	332.2	522.0	921.5
a. Vault Cash of Commercial Banks	5.5			5.5
b. Reserves	19.8			19.8
c. Cash and Deposits	41.2	114.5		155.7
d. Savings and Time Deposits		159.3	179.0	338.3
e. Federal Reserve Float		2.5		2.5
f. Borrowing at Federal Reserve Banks		0.2		0.2
g. Insurance and Pension Reserves			204.6	204.6
h. Finance Company Bonds			16.9	16.9
i. Investment Company Shares			34.3	34.3
j. Mortgage Loans in Process			1.3	1.3
k. Bank Loans, NEC			10.6	10.6
l. Other Loans			18.6	18.6
m. Security Credit			8.5	8.5
n. Taxes Payable			1.1	1.1
o. Miscellaneous and Other	0.8	25.7	47.2	73.7
4. *Net Worth*	0.2	29.5	60.4	90.1

[a]Estimates based on 1958 figures (Goldsmith) plus available capital expenditure and consumption estimates in *Federal Reserve Bulletin*, February 1958 (for years 1959–1966).

[b]Includes deposits in foreign banks.

$$G_T + D_T + BB_T + GB_T = MB_T + MP_T + R_T + DG_T \qquad (6.1)$$

where the subscript T denotes central bank and G = monetary metals (gold), D = deposits of the central banks in the commercial banks, BB = discounts to commercial banks, GB = government securities in the central banks, MB = cash in the vaults of the commercial banks, MP = cash in the hands of the public, R = reserves of the commercial banks, and DG = government deposits in the central banks.

The meaning of most of the variables in equation (6.1) should be clear. The concepts of discounts and reserves will be explained here.

The *discounts* of the central banks to the commercial banks are loans of the central banks to the commercial banks, usually secured with special bank assets such as government bonds, or with securities arising from special types of loans (such as agricultural or industrial loans) made by the commercial banks to the public.

The *reserves* are deposits that the commercial banks are legally obliged to have in the central banks. These deposits must be equal to or larger than a certain proportion of the deposits of the public in commercial banks. The object of this is to make sure that the commercial banks have a certain volume of cash to cover the normal withdrawals from deposit accounts. This cash is in the reserves. In some cases the cash in the vaults of the commercial banks is also accepted as part of their reserves, in addition to deposits in the central banks.

Observe that in the balance equations of the central banks no fixed assets and no net worth have been assumed. The introduction of these two elements only adds to the complexity of the formula and notation.

The main difference between the balance statements of central banks and those of commercial banks has already been observed in the treatment of cash. In addition, since commercial banks deal not only with other banks and government (as the Central Banks do), but also with the public in general, the commercial banks have a larger variety of current assets and liabilities. On the other hand, commercial banks, like central banks, have low levels of net worth and tangible assets.

A consolidated and simplified balance equation of the commercial banks can be expressed as:

$$MB_M + B_M + R_M + A_M = DP_M + BB_M + N_M + D_T \qquad (6.2)$$

where the M subscript denotes commercial banks and MB = cash in vaults of commercial banks, B = loans to the public (households and firms), R = reserves in the central banks, A = fixed assets, DP = deposits from the public, BB = discounts of the central banks, and N = net worth.

The consolidated balance of nonbank financial institutions appears in Table 6–1. To proceed with its study, a more detailed presentation of these institutions is required. A list of them appears in Table 6–2. A brief description of their main assets (uses of funds) and liabilities (sources of funds) appears in Table 6–3.

From Table 6–3 and the previous analysis of banks, it can be seen that the only things that differentiate the "other" financial institutions from each other and from the commercial banks are the particular form of liabilities through which they obtain resources from the public, and the particular financial assets through which they use them. However, the basic characteristic is always maintained; that is, they obtain resources through loans from household savings and they use them for financial assets, lending their resources to other institutions. This characteristic is confirmed for the nonbank financial institutions in the consolidated balance in Table 6–1. Using these observations as justification in the analysis that follows, the commercial banks and the "other" financial institutions will be consolidated under the heading "commercial banks." Equation (6.2) will be interpreted as the consolidated statement of both commercial banks and other financial institutions.

A comparison of equation (6.2) with the actual balance equations for the commercial banks and the nonbank financial institutions in Table 6–1 shows that:

1. On the side of financial assets a large variety of loans (2f–l and o–q in Table 6–1) have been aggregated in loans to the public.
2. On the side of liabilities only those of the commercial banks are considered, that is, demand deposits and discounts. The others, the liabilities of the nonbank financial institutions, are ignored.

To complete this section, the balance equation for the banking system as a whole is obtained from the algebraic sum of equations (6.1) and (6.2) and the fact that

$$BB_T = BB_M$$

$$MB_T = MB_M$$

$$R_T = R_M$$

The consolidated balance equation of the banking system as a whole is

$$G_T + GB_T + B_M + A_M = MP_T + DG_T + DP_M + N_M \qquad (6.3)$$

An important aspect of the consolidated balance equation of the banking system is that it presents the *supply of money* defined as

$$MP_T + DG_T + DP_M$$

Table 6–2
Nonbank Financial Institutions

Saving Institutions	Savings and Loan Associations
	Mutual Saving Banks
	Credit Unions
Insurance	Life Insurance Companies
	Other Insurance Companies
	Private Pension Funds
Finance NEC	Finance Companies
	Security Brokers and Dealers
	Open-End Investment Companies
	Agencies of Foreign Bank

Source: Board of Governors of the Federal Reserve System, *Flow of Funds Accounts, 1945–1967* (February 1968).

that is, as cash in the hands of the public plus demand deposits. This, like any definition, is arbitrary. A question that immediately comes to mind is why the other liabilities of the banking system are excluded. Economists are not in complete agreement about this exclusion. Those who favor it state that the other liabilities of the banking system usually are less liquid, that is, it is easier to exchange cash and deposits for goods and services than to exchange the other liabilities of the banking system for goods and services.

For the analysis of the transactions of the banking system, particularly their relationship with the supply of money, the consolidated balance equations of the public and of the government are needed. It will be assumed here that the balance equation for the public takes the following form:

$$A_P + MP_P + DP_P + GB_P = B_P + N_P \qquad (6.4)$$

where the subscript P denotes public. It should be observed that equation (6.4) can be derived from simplified balance equations obtained from Tables 4–4 and 5–5.

The balance equation for the government has the following form:

$$A_G + DG_G = GB_G + N_G \qquad (6.5)$$

where the subscript G denotes government. Equation (6.5) is the adaptation to the government of equation (2.1) and requires no further explanation. However, the interested reader may refer to Chapter 7 for a more complete discussion of the government.

To complete this section, the initial balance of the financial system to

Table 6–3

Main Assets (Uses of Funds) and Liabilities (Sources of Funds) of Nonbank Financial Institutions

Institution	Assets (Uses of Funds)	Liabilities (Sources of Funds)
Savings and Loan Associations	Mortgage Loans	Savings Accounts Shares Sold
Mutual Savings Banks	Real Estate Loans Government Bonds Corporate Bonds	Time Deposits
Credit Unions	Short-Term Consumer Credit	Shares Sold
Life Insurance Companies	Corporate Bonds Mortgages Government Bonds	Reserves Accumulated from Premiums Income from Investments
Other Insurance Companies (Fire, Casualty)	Corporate Bonds Mortgages Government Bonds	Reserves Accumulated from Premiums Income from Investments
Private Pension Plans (designed to provide income to people after retirement)	Corporate Bonds Mortgages Government Bonds	Contributions of Members
Finance Companies	Corporate Bonds Stocks	Shares Sold Loans

Security Brokers and Dealers	Credit for Purchase
	    of Securities (Margin Accounts)
		Value of Securities
		    Sold not Retired by
		    Sellers
		Profits on Stocks
		    Held by Brokers, not
		    Retired by Owners

Open-End Investment Companies	Corporate Bonds Stock	Shares Sold

Sources: 1. John J. Klein, *Money and the Economy* (Chapter 8) (Chicago: Harcourt Brace and World, Inc., 1965). 2. Herbert B. Dougall, *Capital Markets and Institutions* (Englewood Cliffs: Prentice-Hall, Inc., 1970). 3. John W. Hatard and Millon Christie, *The Investment Business* (New York: Harper and Row, 1964).

be considered as the example for Chapter 6 will be presented in Table 6–7. Only one financial institution is considered in this example. That is to say, no distinction is made between central and commercial banks and between these and other financial institutions.

6.3 Transactions of the Central Banks

A great deal of attention is paid to the transactions of the central banks in the currently accepted theory of the banking system and the money supply, because according to that theory, the transactions of the central banks have a direct impact on the supply of money.

In this section the transactions will only be described. Later, after the currently accepted theory of the banking system and the money supply is presented, it will be shown how, according to that theory, the transactions of the central banks affect the money supply. Finally, the criticism of that theory and the conclusions derived from it will be presented.

The principal transactions of a central bank are:

1. *Open Market Operations.* In these operations the central bank buys or sells bonds or securities to the public. These are usually government securities or bonds.

   Example. The central bank sells bonds for $300 to private dealers (public) on the open market.

2. *Operations with Commercial Banks.* The central bank buys or sells securities or promissory notes from the commercial banks. The most common of these operations are discount operations. The central bank and the commercial bank are the only parties involved in the operation.

   Example. The central bank discounts promissory notes for $500 to a commercial bank. This means that the central bank receives from the commercial bank a promise to pay $500 and gives that amount to the commercial bank in cash.

3. Finally, the central bank performs transactions common to any other bank or firm, that is, it buys labor and materials in the market and receives payments for services such as interest in rediscounts. It also pays interest on the bonds in the hands of the public.

   Example. The central bank buys office materials for $200.

6.4 Transactions of the Commercial Banks

The principal transactions of the commercial banks are:

1. to accept deposits, that is, to sell to a person an obligation on the part of the bank to pay him on demand up to a certain amount of money. Deposit accounts can be increased by actual deposits of cash and checks or with bank loans and payments. They may be decreased by check payments made by the owner of the account. The deposits are a liability of the commercial banks.

2. to lend money, that is, to buy from a person a promise that he will pay to the bank on a future date a fixed amount of money. Loans are assets of the commercial banks.

   Bank loans are frequently made that increase the deposit account

Table 6–4
Examples of Central Bank Transactions

	Tangible Assets		Financial Assets		Liabilities		Net Worth	
	Debit	Credit	Debit	Credit	Debit	Credit	Debit	Credit
Open Market Operations								
Dealers Accounts								
Deposits				300				
Gov Bonds			300					
Commercial Bank Accounts								
Reserves				300				
Deposits Dealers					300			
Central Bank Accounts								
Gov Bonds				300				
Reserves					300			
Discount Operations								
Commercial Bank Accounts								
Reserves			500					
Discounts						500		
Central Bank Accounts								
Reserves						500		
Discounts			500					
Operations Common to Any Other Bank or Firm								
Central Bank (Purchase)								
Inventories	200							
Check Liabilities					200			
Provider Account								
Sales								200
Deposits			200					
Commercial Banks								
Reserves			200					
Deposits Provider						200		
Central Bank								
Check Liability						200		
Reserves					200			

of the person receiving the loan. In this case the loan increases the assets of the commercial banks and the deposits (its liabilities).

The creation of loans is one of the most important operations of the commercial banks because most of their profits come from the interest on these loans.

3. to make deposits in the reserve account. As mentioned earlier, reserves are deposit accounts of the commercial banks in the central bank. These reserves increase with deposits of cash, central bank or government checks made by the commercial banks in the central bank, and decrease with checks drawn by the commercial banks. It should be clear that the reserves are assets of the commercial banks and liabilities of the central bank.

A special characteristic of the reserves is that they have to maintain a certain proportion of the deposits made by the public in the commercial banks. This legal requirement is to insure that the commercial banks will be able to pay on demand the value of the deposits of the public. For this reason, money in the vaults of the commercial banks is sometimes also accepted as legal reserve.

4. to make discounts in the central bank, that is, to receive loans from the central bank. The discounts can be used to increase the reserves of the commercial banks or the cash in their values.

5. to make the usual transactions of a firm, such as buying fixed assets, inventories of raw materials such as paper and pencils, paying employees.

Examples of some of these transactions are presented in the example for chapter 6 in Section 6.7.

6.5 The Currently Accepted Theory of the Relations between Changes in Reserves, Deposits, and Loans of the Commercial Banks, and the Supply of Money

6.5.1 The Textbook Model

The mechanism for the creation of bank deposits will be explained in this section. The following notations will be used:

ΔR = increment in commercial bank reserves in the central bank

ΔDP = increment in deposits of the public

τ = reserve ratio

ΔBB = increment in the loans of the central bank to the commercial banks (assets for the central bank and liabilities for the commercial banks)

ΔB = increment in loans of the commercial banks to the public (assets for the commercial banks and liabilities for the public)

To explain the mechanism of change of deposits assume that the central bank lends to the commercial bank the quantity ΔBB, which the commercial bank uses to increase reserves. As a consequence, the transaction equation for the commercial bank is

$$\Delta R = \Delta BB$$

Assume also that the increased reserve is not needed by the commercial bank because the reserves in existence are sufficient, or, in symbols:

$$R_0 \geq \tau DP_0$$

where the subscript 0 denotes transaction. This means that the commercial bank can use the amount of the loan as it pleases. Assume that since the bank does not want to use it to increase the cash in its vaults, the money will be loaned. As a result, in one transaction the bank transfers reserves to its own values as cash (credit reserves, debit cash), or, in symbols:

$$\Delta MB_0 = \Delta R_0 \tag{6.6}$$

and then lends it to the public (credit cash, debit account receivable);

$$\Delta B_0 = \Delta MB_0 \tag{6.7}$$

This means that all the additional reserve created by the central bank loan is actually lent to the public, that is, from equations (6.6) and (6.7)

$$\Delta R_0 = \Delta B_0 \tag{6.8}$$

A part α of this loan ΔB_0 is deposited in the bank as ΔDP_1, that is,

$$\Delta DP_1 = \alpha \Delta B_0 \tag{6.9}$$

The new deposit ΔDP_1 is used to increase reserves ΔR, the cash in the bank ΔM_1, and for a new loan ΔB_1, that is,

$$\Delta R_1 + \Delta MB_1 + \Delta B_1 = \Delta DP_1 \tag{6.10}$$

assuming that

$$\Delta R_1 = \tau \Delta DP_1$$
$$\Delta MB_1 = \beta \Delta DP_1 \tag{6.11}$$

where β is the proportion of deposits that commercial banks wish to maintain in vaults. It follows from equations (6.10) and (6.11) that

$$\Delta B_1 = (1 - \tau - \beta)\Delta DP_1 \tag{6.12}$$

and from equations (6.8), (6.9), and (6.12) that

$$\Delta B_1 = \alpha(1 - \tau - \beta)\Delta R_0 \qquad (6.13)$$

If a part α of the new loan ΔB_1 is deposited, it follows that

$$\Delta DP_2 = \alpha\Delta B_1 \qquad (6.14)$$

and from equations (6.13) and (6.14) that

$$\Delta DP_2 = \alpha^2(1 - \tau - \beta)\Delta R_0 \qquad (6.15)$$

Now, if the uses of the new deposit are the same as those in equation (6.10), it follows that

$$\Delta R_2 + \Delta MB_2 + \Delta B_2 = \Delta DP_2 \qquad (6.16)$$

With the assumption equation (6.11), we obtain

$$\Delta R_2 = \tau\Delta DP_2$$

$$\Delta MB_2 = \beta\Delta DP_2$$

and

$$\Delta B_2 = (1 - \tau - \beta)DP_2 \qquad (6.17)$$

that is equivalent to equation (6.12). From equations (6.15) and (6.17) we obtain

$$\Delta B_2 = \alpha 2(1 - \tau - \beta)^2 R_0$$

that is equivalent to equation (6.13).

If, again, a part α of the loan ΔB_2 is deposited, we obtain

$$\Delta DP_3 = \alpha\Delta B_2$$

$$= \alpha^2(1 - \tau - \beta)DP_2$$

$$= \alpha^3(1 - \tau - \beta)^2\Delta R_0.$$

and in general if a proportion α of loan n is deposited

$$\Delta DP_{n+1} = \alpha^{n+1}(1 - \tau - \beta)^n R_0$$

The total change in deposits will be

$$\Delta DP = \alpha \sum_{n=1}^{\infty} \alpha^n(1 - \tau - \beta)^n\Delta R_0$$

That is, using the total of an infinite geometric progression

$$\Delta DP = \frac{\alpha\Delta R_0}{1 - \alpha(1 - \tau - \beta)} \qquad (6.18)$$

In equation (6.18) the main elements that influence the expansion of deposits are considered:

1. the reserve ratio τ;
2. the proportion (β) of deposits that the bank wishes to hold in cash in the vaults; and
3. the proportion ($1 - \alpha$) of loans that the public wants to hold in cash.

Only when these three porportions are fixed is it possible to estimate the impact of a change of reserves on deposits. This is why the desires of the public have to be considered among the determinants of the supply of money. Equation (6.18) reduces to

$$\Delta DP = \Delta R/\tau$$

when all the amount loaned is used to open a deposit account ($\alpha = 1$) and all the money that is not used in reserves is loaned again ($\beta = 0$).

At this point it should be observed that the reason the bank does not increase the value of *BB* to infinity is because the money loaned by the central bank has some cost, that is, it reduces the profits of the commercial bank. The bank also wishes to minimize the amount of cash in the vault and its reserves because money loaned is its main source of profits.

6.5.2 The Impact on the Money Supply of the Transactions of the Central Bank, According to the Current Theory

The transactions of the central bank tend to modify the reserves of the commercial banks, and as a result, according to the current theory, they modify the money supply by the amount determined in equation (6.18). The examples in Section 6.3 will be used to study this point in detail.

Example of Open Market Operation. The central bank sells government bonds for $300 to private dealers (public) on the open market. The dealers pay with checks drawn on commercial banks. In this transaction three parties are involved: the dealer, the commercial bank, and the central bank. The recordings of these transactions were presented in Table 6–4.

Observe that the net effect of this operation is a reduction of the commercial bank reserve in an amount equal to the value of the bonds sold to the public. As a result, the commercial banks will tend to reduce deposits to the level determined by equation (6.18).

Example of Operations with Commercial Banks. The central bank discounts promissory notes for $500 to a commercial bank. This means that the central bank receives from the commercial bank a promise to pay $500 and gives that amount to the commercial bank in cash. The commercial bank uses this amount to increase reserves. The recordings of these transactions were presented in Table 6–4.

Observe that the maximum effect that this transaction can have on a supply of money is determined by equation (6.18).

Example of Operations Common to Other Banks or Firms. The central bank buys office materials for $200. Payment is made by check, which is deposited by provider in his deposit account in a commercial bank. The commercial bank uses the check to increase its reserves in the central bank. The supply of money increases in the proportion determined by equation (6.18). The recordings of these transactions appear in Table 6–4.

6.5.3 Instruments to Monetary Policy According to the Current Theory

As a result of the fact that all transactions of the central bank can, in principle (according to the currently accepted theory), affect the supply of money, all of them could be used as *instruments of monetary policy*. However, this title is given mainly to just two types of transactions: (a) open market operations and (b) discount operations.

For obvious reasons, transactions similar to those performed by all firms cannot be used as instruments of monetary policy.

It should also be clear that any changes that can influence the open market and discount operations mentioned above are also instruments of monetary policy. For example, change in the interest paid on discounts is an instrument because it makes discounts more or less attractive. The same is true for the rate of interest paid on bonds used in open market transactions.

Finally, and also for obvious reasons, change in reserve requirements, that is, τ in the earlier notation, is also an instrument of monetary policy.

6.6 Models of the Expansion of the Means of Payment and of Credit

6.6.1 Object of this Section

The limitations of the currently accepted textbook theory of the relations between reserves, deposits, and loans of commercial banks and the supply of money are presented in Section 6.6.2. Using this criticism as a starting point, more acceptable models of the expansion of the means of credit and payment are presented in the following sections.

6.6.2 The Textbook Model of Deposits Expansion: Matrix Formulation and Criticism

To present the simplest textbook explanation of deposits and credit expansion using matrix notation, let

$$B_0 = \begin{bmatrix} \Delta R \\ 0 \end{bmatrix}, \qquad B_t = \begin{bmatrix} L \\ D \end{bmatrix}_t$$

$$T = \begin{bmatrix} 0 & (1-r) \\ a & 0 \end{bmatrix}$$

where L = loans to the public, D = deposits of the public, ΔR = initial and exogenous increment of reserves, r = reserve rate, and a = proportion of the loans that the public keeps in deposits.

With this notation it can be shown easily that

$$\Delta B_t = T^t B_0 \qquad t = 0, \ldots \tag{6.19}$$

and that

$$B = \sum_{t=0}^{\infty} B_t = (I - T)^{-1} B_0 \tag{6.20}$$

where I denotes the appropriate identity matrix.

The system as presented gives the usual elementary description that in step (or period) $2t$, after the initial increment of reserves ΔR in period 0, the banks make loans of size $(1-r)^t a^t \Delta R$, and that the part $(1-r)^t a^{t+1} \Delta R$ is deposited in step $2t + 1$. This means that the entire loan is taken out in cash in period $2t$ and part of it is redeposited in period $2t + 1$. A more reasonable formulation, to be used in Section 6.6.3, is that the whole loan goes into deposits initially, and a portion of it is taken out in cash in the next period.

To complete the presentation of the textbook model, its complement, that is, the model showing cash in the hands of the public and banks, will be presented. This is given by

$$\Delta P_{1t} = T_1 \Delta B_t \tag{6.21}$$

and

$$P_1 = \sum_{t=0}^{\infty} \Delta P_{1t} = T_1 B = \begin{bmatrix} (1-a)/S_1 \\ ra/S_1 \end{bmatrix} \tag{6.22}$$

where

$$P_{1t} = \begin{bmatrix} P_{1p} \\ P_{1b} \end{bmatrix}_t$$

$$T_1 = \begin{bmatrix} (1-a) & 0 \\ 0 & r \end{bmatrix}$$

with $S_1 = \Delta R/[1-a(1-r)]$, P_{1p} denotes cash in the hands of the public as determined by this first model, and P_{1b} denotes cash in the banks as determined by this first model.

A basic limitation of this model, whether in equations (6.19) and (6.20) or in (6.21) and (6.22), is that it includes the assumption that each successive increment of cash in the hands of the public and in reserves is kept separate and can be distinguished from the previous increments and the remaining cash in the economy.

This means that decisions about holding cash and deposits do not take into consideration all the financial resources available to either public or banks. If these totals were considered, the cash in the hands of the public and in banks would be shown by the relationship

$$P_{2t+1} = T_2 P_{2t} \tag{6.23}$$

where P_2 denotes the vector of cash in the hands of the public and in the banks according to this second model, and

$$T_2 = \begin{bmatrix} (1-a) & (1-r) \\ a & r \end{bmatrix}$$

From equation (6.23) it follows that the equilibrium distribution of cash generated by ΔR is

$$P_2 = T_2 P_2 \tag{6.24}$$

that is,

$$P_2 = \begin{bmatrix} (1-r)/S_2 \\ a/S_2 \end{bmatrix}$$

with

$$S_2 = \Delta R/(1+a-r)$$

Another criticism that can be directed at the model in equations (6.19) and (6.20) is that it is centered on the reserve rate. It gives the impression that the existence of a reserve rate is the core of the process of deposit expansion. Again, no attention is paid to the fact that a banking system and deposit accounts can exist and actually have done so without reserves, as long as the money flowing into the banks is sufficient to cover the money flowing out of the banks. This can be seen in the second model, because the equations presented hold with $r = 0$.

The model presented in equations (6.23) and (6.24) is not complete, because the values taken by loans and deposits are not considered. No attempt to do so in a manner similar to equations (6.19) and (6.20) will be made here. Instead, a model dealing simultaneously with money, deposits, and loans will be studied in Section 6.6.3.

6.6.3 A Model Integrating Cash, Deposits, and Loans

Although the main ideas included in the model in equations (6.23) and (6.24) are valid, a model made up of these equations does not explicitly include certain elements that appear in the process of deposit and credit expansion. The following model avoids this objection.

$$
\begin{aligned}
M_{1t+1} &= a_{11}M_{1t} + (1-a_{33})D_t \\
M_{2t+1} &= (1-a_{11})M_{1t} + M_{2t} - (1-a_{33})D_t \\
D_{t+1} &= (1-a_{11})M_{1t} + kM_{2t} + a_{33}D_t - (1-a_{44})L_t \\
L_{t+1} &= kM_{2t} + a_{44}L_t
\end{aligned}
\tag{6.25}
$$

where M_1 = cash in hands of the public, M_2 = cash in the banks, D = deposits, and L = loans.

The system in equation (6.25) can be described as follows: M_{1t+1} is formed with the part of M_{1t} retained plus withdrawals from the banking system. The cash in the banks increases with new deposits, that is, $(1-a_{11})M_{1t}$, and decreases with cash withdrawals, that is, $(1 - a_{33})D_t$. Deposits increase with new deposits, $(1 - a_{11})M_{1t}$, and new loans, kM_{2t}, and decrease with loan payments $(1 - a_{44})L_t$. In the deposits equation it is assumed that loans made do not leave the bank but only increase deposits. The assumption made in this equation with respect to loan payment does not mean that all loans are paid only with cash or with deposits. Regardless of the proportions paid in cash and in deposits, the equation for deposits in equation (6.25) holds. Finally, loans are made in proportion to the cash available in the banks in period t. This assumption represents the banks' attempts to match their resources to the demands on them that are likely to arise. (This point will be treated in greater detail later.)

To simplify presentation, the system in equation (6.25) will be written as follows

$$x_t = Ax_{t-1} \tag{6.26}$$

where the meanings of x and A, derived from equation (6.25) should be clear.

The characteristic equation of the matrix A is

$$(1 - p)^2[p^2 + (1 - a_{11} - a_{33} - a_{44})p$$
$$- (1 - a_{11} - a_{33})a_{44} + k(1 - a_{33})] = 0 \tag{6.27}$$

This equation shows that $p = 1$ is a double characteristic root of the system. The eigen vectors corresponding to this root are

$$g_1' = [1, 0, (1 - a_{11})/(1 - a_{33}), 0]$$

and

$$g_2' = [0, 1, 0, k/(1 - a_{44})]$$

Two additional vectors will correspond to the roots of the quadratic part of equation (6.27).

Since the eigen vectors g_1 and g_2 are linearly independent, the solution of the system in equation (6.25) can be written as follows:

$$x_t = C_1g_1 + C_2g_2 + C_3g_3p_3^t + C_4g_4p_4^t \tag{6.28}$$

where C_i, $i=1,4$, are arbitrary constants; g_i, $i=1,4$, are the eigen vectors of the matrix A; and p_i, $i=1,4$, are the roots of equation (6.27).

To analyze the stability of the model, the absolute values of the p_i have to be specified. To do so the quadratic part of equation (6.27) equated to zero can be written as

$$(p - a_{44})(1 + p - a_{11} - a_{33}) = -k(1 - a_{33}) \tag{6.29}$$

If all the coefficients a_{ii}, $i = 1,3,4$, lie between zero and one, the right-hand side of equation (6.29) is negative. As a result, the left-hand side of equation (6.29) must also be negative, that is, its two factors must differ in sign. This is the case if and only if $|p_i| < 1$. In this case equation (6.29) shows that the system in equation (6.25) approaches an "equilibrium value" characterized by

$$x = C_1g_1 + C_2g_2 \tag{6.30}$$

To obtain additional information on the equilibrium value of the vector

x, it should be observed that the following conditions must be satisfied. First, from the eigen vectors g_1 and g_2 it follows that

$$(1 - a_{11})M_1 = (1 - a_{33})D \qquad (6.31)$$

and

$$kM_2 = (1 - a_{44})L \qquad (6.32)$$

where the variables without time subscript are the components of the equilibrium vector x. Next,

$$M = M_1 + M_2 \qquad (6.33)$$

where M is the total amount of cash available, and, finally,

$$D = M_2 + L \qquad (6.34)$$

This last equation is derived from the following ones:

$$D = \sum_t [(1 - a_{11})M_{1t} - (1 - a_{44})L_t + kM_{2t} - (1 - a_{33})D_t]$$

$$L = \sum_t [kM_{2t} - (1 - a_{44})L_t]$$

and

$$M_2 = \sum_t [(1 - a_{11})M_{1t} - (1 - a_{33})D_t]$$

Equations (6.31) to (6.34) can be used to express the components of the equilibrium vector x as functions of the components of the matrix A and those of M.

It is interesting to note that, while the matrix of the system in equation (6.25) is irreducible, the equilibrium of the system can be broken down into the separate portfolio equilibria of the banks and the public. This suggests a qualitative difference between the system's complexity in equilibria and disequilibrium, which could be an object of further research.

The model in equation (6.25) can easily be extended to include bank reserves. For this, M_2 must be redefined to mean cash that the banks can use, while reserves R are cash that the banks cannot use, even though the banks continue to hold it. The equation corresponding to M_2 is also modified to include the term $- r(D_{t+1} - D_t)$, meaning that an amount of cash equal to a proportion r of the increments in deposits must be held as a reserve. Finally, an equation for R is introduced, making reserves equal to their past values plus the increments specified by the additional deposits. The introduction of these modifications does not change any of the basic characteristics of the model or its conclusions. This result is reasonable, since it is intuitively clear that no reserves are required when deposits and withdrawals are deterministic. On the other hand, if there were a stochastic element involved in either or both of them, some reserves would be required.

It is also possible to modify the model to assume that new loans $L_{t+1} - a_{44}L_t$ depend not only on kM_{2t} but instead on $k(M_{2t} - bL_t)$, that is, on the difference between cash in the banks and a proportion of unpaid loans last period. In this case, the demand–supply of new loans is made to depend not entirely on the banks' resources, but also to some extent on those of the public.

From a mathematical point of view, this model and the one in equation (6.25) are formally identical. To see this, observe that the current assumption can be incorporated using $a_{44} - kb$ instead of a_{44} in the equation for D_{t+1} and L_{t+1} in equation (6.25). If $a_{44} > kb$, the conclusions still hold. However, if $a_{44} < kb$, the system will be stable whenever $-1 < a_{44} - kb$. Otherwise, some cases of instability might exist. These conclusions show that the total of standing loans should be larger than the weight given to the loans in the reduction of new loans. In other terms, a too-cautious attitude of banks with respect to loans might upset the stability of the system.

6.6.4 Nonbank Financial Liabilities and the Supply of Money

It can be concluded from the analysis of the model in equation (6.25) that the capacity to create means of payment is not limited to commercial banks and financial institutions. It is also enjoyed by any economic unit able to sell the financial liabilities it issues. These liabilities must be able to serve as means of payments to the rest of the economy, and each economic unit issuing liabilities must be able to sell more of its liabilities than its absorbs as payments from the rest of the economy. This can be seen more explicitly in the following model:

$$M_{1t+1} = a_{11}M_{1t} + (1 - a_{22})M_{2t} + (1 - a_{33})U_{1t} - (1 - a_{44})U_{2t}$$

$$M_{2t+1} = (1 - a_{11})M_{1t} + a_{22}M_{2t} - (1 - a_{33}U_{1t} + (1 - a_{44})U_{2t}$$

$$U_{1t+1} = k_1M_{2t} + a_{33}U_{1t}$$

$$U_{2t+1} = k_2M_{1t} + a_{44}U_{2t}$$

$$(6.35)$$

where M_i denotes money in the hands of economic units of type i, $i = 1,2;$

and U_i denotes financial liabilities issued by economic unit $j \neq i$, and accepted by economic unit i, $i = 1,2$.

According to the model in equation (6.35), the economic units i make direct payments in cash to the economic units j and, in addition, make payments to redeem part of the financial liabilities they have issued. Also, economic units i issue financial liabilities in proportion to the money they have available, and these liabilities are bought by economic units j.

In the case of equation (6.35), 1 is again a characteristic root of the matrix of the system. However, in the present case it is not repeated. The equilibrium eigen vector takes the form

$$\left[1, \frac{(1-a_{11} + k_2)}{(1-a_{22} + k_1)}, \frac{(1-a_{11} + k_2)k_1}{(1-a_{33})(1-a_{22} + k_1)}, \frac{k_2}{(1-a_{44})} \right]$$

This vector shows that the means of payment used by the two economic units considered are larger than the money available to them.

6.6.5 Equilibrium of the System, Total Payments, and the Sector Velocities of Circulation of Cash and Deposits

It should be clear that, with minor modifications, the models in Sections 6.6.3 and 6.6.4 can be expanded to include any number of sectors and/or means of payment. No attempt will be made here to present a general form of either of these models. However, an extension of the model in Section 6.6.4 is presented, because it makes it possible to study the total payments made by the different economic units and to define precisely the velocity of money and of deposits. The extended model takes the following form:

$$M_{1t+1} = a_{11}M_{1t} + a_{12}M_{2t} + \quad a_{14}D_{1t}$$

$$M_{2t+1} = a_{21}M_{1t} + a_{22}M_{2t} + \quad a_{25}D_{2t}$$

$$M_{3t+1} = a_{31}M_{1t} + a_{32}M_{2t} + \quad M_{3t} - a_{14}D_{1t} - a_{25}D_{2t}$$

$$D_{1t+1} = a_{31}M_{1t} \quad + k_1M_{3t} + a_{44}D_{1t} + a_{45}D_{2t} - (1-a_{66})L_{1t}$$

$$D_{2t+1} = \quad a_{32}M_{2t} + k_2M_{3t} + a_{54}D_{1t} + a_{55}D_{2t} \quad - (1-a_{77})L_{2t}$$

$$L_{1t+1} = \quad k_1M_{3t} + \quad a_{66}L_{1t}$$

$$L_{2t+1} = \quad k_2M_{3t} + \quad a_{77}L_{2t}$$

$$(6.36)$$

where M_i denotes cash $i = 1,2$ in nonbank sectors, $i = 3$ in banks; D_i denotes deposits of sector i; and L_i denotes bank loans to sector i.

The meanings of the equations follow as a direct extension of those in the model in Section 6.6.3. For this reason they will not be explained in detail. It also follows that

$$\sum_i a_{ij} = 1 \qquad j = 1,5 \tag{6.37}$$

Using equation (6.37) it can be shown that 1 is a triple characteristic root of the matrix of the system in equation (6.36). The following three linearly independent eigen vectors correspond to this root:

$$g_1 = (y_1, y_2, 0, y_4, y_5, 0, 0)$$

$$g_2 = (0, 0, 1, 0, 0, k_1/(1 - a_{66}), 0)$$

and

$$g_3 = [0, 0, 1, 0, 0, 0, k_2/(1 - a_{77})]$$

where the formulas for the y_i can be easily derived by solving the system $g_1 = Ag_1$.

To study the total payments generated by a system like the one described by equation (6.36), assume that V_0 is a vector of initial conditions. Then $V_1 = AV_0$, given the total means of payment available to the different sectors after one period. The total of payments made in passing from date 0 to date 1 is

$$Y_1 = V_1 - BV_0 \tag{6.38}$$

where we have the matrix equation in Figure 6–1.

It can be shown by induction that the payments between dates t and $t + 1$ are

$$Y_{t+1} = (A - B)A^t V_0$$

From this it follows that, if the initial vector V_0 is an equilibrium vector, total payments in N periods will be given by

$$N(A - B)V_0 \tag{6.39}$$

This means that the components of the matrix $N(A-B)$ are the sector velocities of circulation of money and deposits.

Table 6–5
Example for Chapter 6: Record of the Transactions of Banking Institutions

Concept	Tangible Assets		Financial Assets		Liabilities		Net Worth	
	+Debit	–Credit	+Debit	–Credit	–Debit	+Credit	–Debit	+Credit
1. Bk Sells Services to Ind								34.8
Deposits Ind					25.0			
Cash Ind					9.8			
2a. Inventory Raw Materials Ind	6.0							
Deposits Ind						4.0		
Cash Ind						2.0		
2b. Capital Ind	5.9							
Deposits Ind						5.9		
3. Bk Sells Services to Hh								10.1
Deposits Hh					7.0			
Cash Hh					2.0			
Accounts Receivable			1.1					
4a. Interest to Hh							12.4	
Deposits Hh						9.0		
Cash Hh						3.4		
4b. Wages to Hh							14.6	
Deposits Hh						10.0		
Cash Hh						4.6		
5. Capital RW	1.1							
Deposits RW						1.1		
6. Profits to Hh							1.4	
Deposits Hh						1.4		
7a. Production of Services							7.0	
Use of Raw Materials		7.0						
7b. Production of Services							0.1	
Use of Raw Materials		0.1						

#	Account	(1)	(2)	(3)	(4)	(5)	(6)
8.	Use Capital		1.1				
	Depreciate						
9a.	Services Purchased to RW					1.1	
	Deposits RW				0.3	0.3	
9b.	Inventory Raw Materials RW						
	Deposits RW	0.1			0.1		
10a.	Services Sold Gov						1.2
	Deposits Gov			1.2			
10b.	Services Sold RW						0.4
	Deposits RW			0.4			
11a.	Deposits Hh			10.0			
	Deposits Ind				10.0		
11b.	Deposits Hh			250.0			
	Deposits Ind				250.0		
11c.	Deposits Hh			90.0			
	Deposits Ind				90.0		
11d.	Deposits Hh			25.0			
	Deposits Ind				25.0		
11e.	Deposits Hh			23.2			
	Deposits Ind				23.2		
11f.	Deposits Hh			8.0			
	Deposits Gov				8.0		
11g.	Deposits Hh			105.0			
	Deposits Gov				105.0		
11h.	Deposits Hh			2.1			
	Deposits RW				2.1		
11i.	Deposits Hh			10.0			
	Deposits Ind				10.0		
12a.	Deposits Ind			400.0			
	Deposits Hh				400.0		

Table 6–5 (cont.)

Concept	Tangible Assets		Financial Assets		Liabilities		Net Worth	
	+Debit	−Credit	+Debit	−Credit	−Debit	+Credit	−Debit	+Credit
12b. Deposits Ind Deposits Hh					15.0	15.0		
12c. Deposits Ind Deposits Gov					60.0	60.0		
12d. Deposits Ind Deposits RW					35.0	35.0		
12e. Deposits Ind Deposits Hh					25.0	25.0		
12f. Deposits Ind Deposits Hh					13.0	13.0		
12g. Deposits Ind Deposits RW					8.0	8.0		
13. Tax to Gov Deposits Gov Cash Gov						4.0 1.9	5.9	
14a. Deposits Gov Deposits Hh					35.0	35.0		
14b. Deposits Gov Deposits Ind					85.0	85.0		
14c. Deposits Gov Deposits RW					2.1	2.1		
14d. Deposits Gov Deposits Hh					15.0	15.0		

15a.	Deposits RW		10.0	10.0
	Deposits Ind			
15b.	Deposits RW		1.5	1.5
	Deposits Ind			
15c.	Deposits RW		2.1	2.1
	Deposits Ind			
15d.	Deposits RW		4.0	4.0
	Deposits Hh			
15e.	Deposits RW		1.7	1.7
	Deposits Hh			
15f.	Deposits RW		1.1	1.1
	Deposits Hh			
15g.	Deposits RW		2.5	2.5
	Deposits Ind			
15h.	Deposits RW		6.0	6.0
	Deposits Gov			
15i.	Deposits RW		4.7	4.7
	Deposits Ind			
15j.	Deposits RW		2.0	2.0
	Deposits Hh			
16.	Deposits Hh Withdrawal		20.0	20.0
	Cash to Hh			
17.	Gov Bonds Sold Bk	5.0		
	Deposits Hh		5.0	5.0
18.	Securities		5.0	5.0
	Deposits Hh			
19.	Shares		3.0	3.0
	Deposits Hh			

Table 6–5 (cont.)

		Tangible Assets		Financial Assets		Liabilities		Net Worth	
	Concept	+Debit	−Credit	+Debit	−Credit	−Debit	+Credit	−Debit	+Credit
20.	Deposits Hh					25.0	25.0		
	Cash Hh								
21.	Gov Bonds from Hh			5.0			5.0		
	Deposits Hh								
22.	Deposits Ind					5.0	5.0		
	Cash Ind								
23.	Deposits Ind					10.0	10.0		
	Cash Ind								
24.	Accounts Receivable Ind			5.0			5.0		
	Deposits Ind								
25.	Gold RW				10.0	10.0			
	Deposits RW								
	Total	13.1	8.2	11.1	15.0	1380.4	1377.7	42.8	46.5

$$B = \begin{bmatrix} a_{11} & 0 & 0 & a_{14} & 0 & 0 & 0 \\ 0 & a_{22} & 0 & 0 & a_{25} & 0 & 0 \\ a_{31} & a_{32} & 1 & -a_{14} & -a_{25} & 0 & 0 \\ a_{31} & 0 & k_1 & a_{44} & 0 & -(1-a_{66}) & 0 \\ 0 & a_{32} & k_2 & 0 & a_{55} & 0 & -(1-a_{77}) \\ 0 & 0 & k_1 & 0 & 0 & a_{66} & 0 \\ 0 & 0 & k_2 & 0 & 0 & 0 & a_{77} \end{bmatrix}$$

Figure 6–1. Matrix B in Equation (6.38)

The matrix $N(A-B)$ in equation (6.39) takes the form

$$\begin{bmatrix} 0 & Na_{12} & 0 & 0 & 0 & 0 \\ Na_{12} & 0 & 0 & 0 & 0 & 0 \\ 0 & 0 & 0 & 0 & 0 & 0 \\ 0 & 0 & 0 & 0 & Na_{45} & 0 \\ 0 & 0 & 0 & Na_{54} & 0 & 0 \\ 0 & 0 & 0 & 0 & 0 & 0 \\ 0 & 0 & 0 & 0 & 0 & 0 \end{bmatrix}$$

in the case under consideration.

From this it follows that the product

$$\begin{bmatrix} 1 & 0 & 0 & 1 & 0 & 0 & 0 \\ 0 & 1 & 0 & 0 & 1 & 0 & 0 \end{bmatrix} N(A - B)V_0$$

constitutes the matrices C' and D' in the generalized equation of exchange (GEE) for an economy with only two sectors. This GEE is presented in Chapter 11.

6.7 Example for Chapter 6: Transactions of the Banking System

Examples of some of the transactions of central and commercial banks appear here in the example for Chapter 6. Transactions dealing with operations between one financial institution and another are not considered, because only one financial institution is used in the example.

The detailed record of the transactions in the example for this chapter is presented in Table 6–5.

1. Banks receive $34.80 payment for services provided to industry: $25 paid by check, $9.80 in cash (TR 2, 6, a).

2. Banks purchase from industry:

    (a) Raw materials for $6: $4 paid increasing industry deposits, $2.00 in cash (TR 2, 10, a);

    (b) Capital goods for $5.90: paid increasing industry deposits (TR 2, 10, b).

3. Banks receive $10.10 from Hh as payment for services provided: $7 paid reducing Hh deposit account, $2 in cash, $1.10 credit (TR 1, 4, a).

4. Banks pay to Hh:

    (a) Interest of $12.40: $9 paid increasing Hh deposit account, and $3.40 in cash (TR 1, 7, a);

    (b) Wages of $14.60: $10 paid increasing Hh deposit account, $4.60 in cash (TR 1, 8, a).

5. Banks purchase capital goods from RW for $1.10: paid increasing RW deposits (TR 5, 6, b).

6. Banks pay $1.40 as profits to Hh: paid increasing Hh deposit account (TR 1, 9).

7. Banks use in the production of their services:

    (a) Raw materials from industry with a value of $7.00

    (b) Imported raw materials with a value of $0.10

8. The capital goods of banks depreciate by $1.10

9. Homeland banks pay to:

    (a) RW Bk $0.30 for services provided: paid increasing RW deposits (TR 5, 8, a);

    (b) RW Ind $0.10 for raw materials and to refill inventories: paid increasing RW deposits (TR 5, 8, b).

10. Banks sell services to:

    (a) Gov for $1.20: paid decreasing Gov deposit account (TR 4, 4);

    (b) RW for $0.40: paid decreasing RW deposit account (TR 5, 9).

11. Households deposit the following checks:

    (a) From Ind for $10 (TR 1, 1, a; TR 2, 4, a);

    (b) From Ind for $250 (TR 1, 1, b; TR 2, 4, b);

(c) From Ind for $90 (TR 1, 1, c; TR 2, 4, c);

(d) From Ind for $25 (TR 1, 1, d; TR 2, 7, a);

(e) From Ind for $23.20 (TR 1, 1, e; TR 2, 8, a);

(f) From Gov for $8 (TR 1, 7, b; TR 4, 3, a);

(g) From Gov for $105 (TR 1, 8, b, TR 4, 3, b);

(h) From RW for $2.10 (TR 1, 8, c; TR 5, 7);

(i) From Ind for $10 (TR 1, 13; TR 2, 16).

12. Industry deposits the following checks:

(a) From Hh for $400 (TR 1, 2, a; TR 2, 10, c);

(b) From Hh for $15 (TR 1, 2, b; TR 2, 10, d);

(c) From Gov for $60 (TR 2, 10, e; TR 4, 2);

(d) From RW for $35 (TR 2, 10, f; TR 5, 4);

(e) From Hh for $25 (TR 1, 11, c; TR 2, 14);

(f) From Hh for $13 (TR 1, 11, f; TR 2, 15);

(g) From RW for $8 (TR 2, 18; TR 5, 14).

13. Banks pay taxes of $5.90: $4 paid increasing Government deposit account, $1.90 in cash (TR 4, 1, c).

14. Government deposits the following checks:

(a) From Hh for $35 (TR 1, 6; TR 4, 1, a);

(b) From Ind for $85 (TR 2, 9; TR 4, 1, b);

(c) From RW for $2.10 (TR 4, 1, d; TR 5, 10);

(d) From Hh for $15 (TR 1, 11, a; TR 4, 6).

15. Rest of the world deposits the following checks:

(a) HL Ind for $10 (TR 2, 1; TR 5, 1);

(b) HL Ind for $1.50 (TR 2, 7, b; TR 5, 2);

(c) HL Ind for $2.10 (TR 2, 8, b; TR 5, 3);

(d) HL Hh for $4 (TR 1, 3, a; TR 5, 3, a);

(e) HL Hh for $1.70 (TR 1, 3, b; TR 5, 3, b);

(f) HL Hh for $1.10 (TR 1, 4, a; TR 5, 3, c);

(g) HL Ind for $2.50 (TR 2, 12; TR 5, 6, a);

(h) HL Gov for $6 (TR 4, 5; TR 5, 11);

(i) HL Ind for $4.70 (TR 2, 13; TR 5, 12);

(j) HL Hh for $2 (TR 1, 11, e; TR 5, 13).

16. Households withdraw $20 from their deposit account (TR 1, 10).

17. Households buy Gov bonds from Bk for $5: paid reducing Hh deposit account (TR 1, 11, b).

18. Households buy securities from Bk for $5: paid reducing Hh deposit account (TR 1, 11, d).
19. Banks sell shares to Hh for $3: paid reducing Hh deposit account (TR 1, 11, g).
20. Households deposit $25 in their deposit account (TR 1, 12).
21. Banks buy $5 of Gov bonds from Hh: paid increasing Hh deposit account (TR 1, 14).
22. Industry withdraws $5 from its deposit account (TR 2, 17).
23. Industry deposits $10 in its deposit account (TR 2, 19).
24. Banks lend $5 to Ind: paid increasing Ind deposit account (TR 2, 20).
25. Banks transfer gold valued at $10 to RW. Gold in this case is considered a financial asset. Banks reduce RW deposit accounts (TR 5, 15).

It should be clear from the description of the recording of the transactions presented here that the principles in Chapters 1 and 2 are applied without modification to the financial institutions. The only point that deserves special attention is the special forms taken by their financial assets and liabilities. The fact that money is a liability of the central bank is particularly likely to create confusion when recording bank transactions.

6.8 The Transactions Statement for Financial Institutions

The transactions statement derived from Table 6–5 is presented in Table 6–6. The treatment of deposits in this statement has one special characteristic. Not all the amounts deposited or withdrawn from the banks are included, but only the following: (a) those in which some cash is deposited in or withdrawn from the bank; (b) those in which a payment is made for bank services, or in which the bank pays for services provided to it; and (c) those in which deposits are increased by means of a bank loan or decreased by a payment of a loan. In summary, only transactions 1 to 6, 9, 10, 13, and 16 to 25 are included among deposits in Table 6–6. The other transactions represent only transfers from one deposit account to another, and do not appear in the transactions statement for banks in Table 6–6, but they do appear in Table 6–7.

Transfers from one deposit account to another do not appear in the transactions statement for banks to be used in the detailed national transaction table because they are already recorded in the transactions of the two nonbank economic units that make the transaction that results in the transfer of deposit. To record them in the bank accounts as well would result in double accounting.

For additional information on the transactions statement for the financial system, the reader should refer to Chapter 10, Table 10–3, columns (6) and (7), where the transactions statement for the financial institutions in the United States in 1966 is presented. This statement is obtained from

Table 6–6
Example for Chapter 6: Transactions Statement for the Banking System

	Debit	Credit
Tangible Assets		
Purchases Capital		
Ind	5.9	
RW	1.1	
Capital Consumption		1.1
Inventories of Raw Materials		
Ind	6.0	7.0
RW	0.1	0.1
Financial Assets and Liabilities		
Cash		
Hh	27.0	28.0
Ind	19.8	7.0
Gov		1.9
Deposits[a]		
Hh	40.0	50.4
Ind	20.0	24.9
Gov	1.2	4.0
RW	10.4	1.5
Other		
Hh	6.1	13.0
Ind	5.0	—
Gov	—	—
RW	—	10.0
Total Assets and Liabilities	152.6	148.9
Net Worth		
Sales		
Hh		10.1
Ind		34.8
Gov		1.2
RW		0.4
Purchases HL Ind	6.0	
Purchases RW	0.4	
Change Inventory Ind	1.0	
Depreciation	1.1	
Wages Hh	14.6	
Interest Hh	12.4	
Profits Hh	1.4	
Tax	5.9	
Total Net Worth	42.8	46.5
Profit and Loss	3.7	
Total	195.4	195.4

[a]Deposits are presented in this statement in the form required for the detailed national transactions statement in Table 10–1.

Table 6–7

Example for Chapter 6: Summary of the Accounting Process of the Banking System

Accounts (1)	Initial Balance Debit (2)	Credit (3)	Transactions Statement Debit (4)	Credit (5)	Income Statement Debit (6)	Credit (7)	Final Balance Debit (8)	Credit (9)
Tangible Assets								
Land/Structures	23.3						23.3	
Equipment	15.2		7.0	1.1			21.1	
Inventory Raw Materials	6.5		6.1	7.1			5.5	
Financial Assets								
Gold and Foreign Exchange	16.9			10.0			6.9	
Accounts Receivable	9.1		6.1				15.2	
Securities	173.6						173.6	
Shares	258.6						258.6	
Gov Bonds	93.5		5.0	5.0			93.5	
Liabilities								
Cash		146.8	46.8	36.9				136.9
Deposits		288.9	1,341.6	1,340.8				288.1
Accounts Payable		70.8						70.8
Shares		64.7		3.0				67.7
Securities				5.0				5.0
Net Worth		25.5						29.2
Services Provided				46.5		46.5		
Change Inventory			1.0		1.0			
Wages			14.6		14.6			
Depreciation			1.1		1.1			
Purchases Ind HL			6.0		6.0			
Purchases RW			0.4		0.4			
Interest Hh HL			12.4		12.4			
Distributed Profits			1.4		1.4			
Tax			5.9		5.9			
Nondistributed Profits					3.7			
Total	596.7	596.7	1,455.4	1,455.4	46.5	46.5	597.7	597.7

the aggregation and consolidation of all the transactions of the subsectors considered.

6.9 Income and Product Statement

Income and product equations of the central and commercial banks are based on the same principles as those of other firms and will not be described in detail here. The income and product statement derived from

Table 6–6 is presented in Table 6–7, columns (6) and (7). The statement obtained for Table 10–3 appears in the bottom part of that table.

6.10 Summary of the Accounting Process for the Financial Sector

The summary of the accounting process derived from the initial balance and the transactions and income statements is presented in Table 6–7. As before, this summary is obtained by applying principles explained in Chapters 2 and 3.

References

Brovedani, B., *Un Modelo de Analisis Monetario y de Programacion Financiera* (Chapter 2) (Mexico: Centro de Estudios Monetarios Latino Americanos, 1969).

Dougall, H. B., *Capital Markets and Institutions* (Englewood Cliffs, New Jersey: Prentice Hall, 1970).

Hatard, J. W., and Christie, M., *The Investment Business* (New York: (Harper and Row, 1969).

Klein, J. J., *Money and the Economy* (Chapter 8) (Chicago: Harcourt and Brace World, Inc., 1965).

Lyle, E. F., "Commercial Banks," in Williams, R., and Doris, L. (eds.), *Encyclopedia of Accounting Systems* (Englewood Cliffs, New Jersey: Prentice Hall Inc., 1964) (7th printing).

Mathews, R., *Accounting for Economists* (Chapter 18) (London: Angus and Robertson, 1969).

Powelson, J., *Economic Accounting* (Chapter 13) (New York: McGraw Hill, 1955).

7 The Government Accounting System

7.1 Purpose of This Chapter

In order to simplify presentation, government will be considered here as a single accounting unit. In practice, however, almost all countries, with or without a federal organization, contain several levels of government, and, with the exception of the national level, each level includes several units. For example, many countries have, in addition to the national government, several state and even more city governments. Each of these units keeps separate accounts.

The presentation here deals with a consolidated account including all the regional and local governments, together with the national government. This consolidation is seldom used for administrative purposes. It appears only in the national accounts.

On the other hand, enterprises belonging to the government and producing goods and services that are sold to the public in a manner similar to that of any other private enterprise are excluded from the government sector considered in the macro-accounts. These enterprises are included in the production sector of the economy.

The accounting process for the national and regional governments does not differ from that of households, firms, or financial institutions. The same basic statements are considered, and the same rules for their use are maintained.

The consolidation of the different government units also follows the principle of consolidation used for all other sectors, that is, the debits (credits) in the accounts of one government unit that also appear as credits (debits) in another government unit cancel each other out. This is why government is treated as one single unit here. The accounts of this unit follow according to the methods used in the previous chapters.

7.2 Balance Equation for the Government

An example of the balance statement for the U.S. Government is presented in Chapter 9, Table 9–1. It should be observed that the government debt, listed as U.S. government securities and state and local obligations, is larger than the total assets of the government. As a result, the government presents a negative net worth. This means that the government owes more than it owns, a fact that is somewhat surprising. In the case of any private organization, this situation would result in bankruptcy. Actually this is an indication of the rather conventional nature of accounting. Part of the reason for the negative net worth of the government is that public property, such as highways and harbors, is not included in the balance statement. This is mainly due to the difficulty in determining their value.

The balance statement for the government account in the example for Chapter 7 is presented later in this chapter in Table 7–3, columns (2) and (3).

7.3 Government Transactions

Government transactions are the operations by means of which the government obtains resources or uses them.

The government obtains resources mainly through taxation of firms, banks, and households, and by increasing the public debt. It is a characteristic of the government that it does not obtain resources by selling its output in the market. Tax payments received by the government are recorded as credits to net worth. Following the standard procedure, these are recorded under their specific names, that is, as taxes. The recording of changes in public debt does not have any special characteristics. Increments in public debt are credits, while reductions are debits to government liabilities.

The government uses resources to buy goods and services and to pay interest on the public debt. To simplify, in the following analysis it will be assumed that all goods bought by the government are immediately consumed. This avoids the need to take into consideration the accumulation of inventories and their use in the production of government services. In certain cases it might be correct to consider that the government accumulates inventories, and that they are gradually used during normal government operations. If so, the accounts would be similar to those of a firm producing services. On the basis of these observations, the payments for goods are debits to net worth. Similar treatment is given to payments for services and for interest on the public debt. In all these cases, payments are recorded under their own names.

Examples of the transactions mentioned appear in the example for Chapter 7:

1. Government receives tax payments:

   (a) From Hh, $75.20: $35 paid by check, $40.20 in cash (TR 1, 6; TR 3, 14, a);

(b) From Ind, $91.60: $85 paid by check, $6.60 in cash (TR 2, 9,; TR 3, 14, b);

(c) From Bk, $5.90: $4 paid increasing government deposits, $1.90 in cash (TR 3, 13);

(d) From RW, $2.10: paid by check (TR 3, 14, c; TR 5, 10).

2. Government purchases consumption goods for $74.50 from Ind: $60 paid by check, $10 in cash, $4.50 credit. Goods are consumed immediately (TR 2, 10, e; TR 3, 12, d).

3. Government pays to Hh:

(a) Interest of $9.90: $8 paid by check, $1.90 in cash (TR 1, 7, b; TR 3, 11, f);

(b) Wages of $117.80: $105 paid by check, $12.80 in cash (TR 1, 8, b; TR 3, 11, g).

4. Government purchases services from Bk for $1.20: paid decreasing Gov deposit account (TR 3, 10, a).

5. Government purchases consumption goods from RW for $7.50: $6 paid by check, $1.50 credit. Goods are consumed immediately (TR 3, 15, h; TR 5, 11).

6. Government sells bonds to Hh for $15: paid by check (TR 1, 11, a; TR 3, 14, d).

The record of the transactions in the example for Chapter 7 appears in Table 7–1.

7.4 The Government Transactions Statement

The transactions statement is derived from the record of transactions in the manner described in the previous chapters. The statement obtained for the example for Chapter 7 appears in Table 7–2.

The government transactions statement is equivalent to a consolidation of the receipts and expenditures of national, regional, and local governments. This statement is called "government receipts and expenditures." An example appears in Chapter 10, Table 10–3, columns (8) and (9), for the U.S. government in 1966.

If all receipts and expenditures of the government budgets were actually realized, the statement of government receipts and expenditures would also be equal to a consolidation of all national, regional, and local budgets. However, the budgets are very seldom, if ever, realized in all their details.

Table 7–1
Example for Chapter 7: Record of Government Transactions

Concept	Tangible Assets		Financial Assets		Liabilities		Net Worth	
	+Debit	−Credit	+Debit	−Credit	−Debit	+Credit	−Debit	+Credit
1a. Tax Receipts Hh								75.2
Deposits Hh			35.0					
Cash Hh			40.2					
1b. Tax Ind								91.6
Deposits Ind			85.0					
Cash Ind			6.6					
1c. Tax Bk								5.9
Deposits			4.0					
Cash			1.9					
1d. Tax RW								2.1
Deposits RW			2.1					
2. Consumption Goods Ind							74.5	
Deposits Ind				60.0				
Cash Ind				10.0				
Accounts Payable Ind						4.5		
3a. Interest Hh							9.9	
Deposits Hh				8.0				
Cash Hh				1.9				
3b. Wages Hh							117.8	
Deposits Hh				105.0				
Cash Hh				12.8				
4. Bank Services							1.2	
Deposits Gov				1.2				
5. Consumption RW							7.5	
Deposits RW				6.0				
Accounts Payable RW						1.5		
6. Gov Bonds Hh						15.0		
Deposits Hh			15.0					
Total			189.8	204.9		21.0	210.9	174.8

Table 7–2
Example for Chapter 7: Government Transactions Statement

	Debit	Credit
Tangible Assets		
Purchases Capital		
Financial Assets and Liabilities		
Cash		
Hh	40.2	14.7
Ind	6.6	10.0
Bk	1.9	—
Deposits		
Hh	50.0	113.0
Ind	85.0	60.0
Bk	4.0	1.2
RW	2.1	6.0
Other		
Hh	—	15.0
Ind	—	4.5
RW		1.5
Total Assets and Liabilities	189.8	225.9
Net Worth		
Tax		
Hh		75.2
Ind		91.6
Bk		5.9
RW		2.1
Consumption Goods and Services		
Ind	74.5	
Bk	1.2	
RW	7.5	
Wages	117.8	
Interest	9.9	
Total Net Worth	210.9	174.8
Total	400.7	400.7

7.5 Government Income and Product Statement

The income and product statement for the government, usually called
"income originating in government," is equal to credits minus debits in all
the accounts affecting net worth. This means it is evaluated in the same
way as the income statement of any other accounting unit. The results obtained from the transactions statement in Table 7–2 appear in Table 7–3.
The income statement for the U.S. Government evaluated from the data
in Table 10–3 appears at the bottom of that table.

Table 7–3

Example for Chapter 7: Summary of the Government's Accounting Process

Accounts (1)	Initial Balance Debit (2)	Credit (3)	Transactions Statement Debit (4)	Credit (5)	Income and Product Debit (6)	Credit (7)	Final Balance Debit (8)	Credit (9)
Tangible Assets								
Land/Structures	40.6						40.6	
Equipment	60.3						60.3	
Inventory Raw Materials								
Financial Assets								
Cash	26.4		48.7	24.7			50.4	
Deposits	68.9		141.1	180.2			29.8	
Liabilities								
Bonds		215.0		15.0				230.0
Accounts Payable				6.0				6.0
Net Worth		−18.8						−54.9
Tax Receipts				174.8		174.8		
Consumption Goods and Services			83.2		83.2			
Wages			117.8		117.8			
Interest			9.9		9.9			
Deficit						36.1		
Totals	196.2	196.2	400.7	400.7	210.9	210.9	181.1	181.1

7.6 Summary of the Government Accounting Process

The summary of the government accounting process, including initial balance, transactions statement, income and product statement, and final balance, appears in Table 7–3.

References

Enthoven, A. J. H., *Accountancy and Economic Development Policy* (Chapter 4) (Amsterdam: North Holland/American Elsevier, 1973).

Mathews, R., *Accounting for Economists* (Chapters 8, 18) (London: Angus and Robertson, 1969).

Powelson, J., *Economics Accounting* (Chapter 16) (New York: McGraw Hill, 1955).

8

The Accounting System of the Rest of the World

8.1 Content of This Chapter

The *rest of the world* (RW) is an aggregation of all the countries of the world, except homeland (HL). To simplify presentation, it is considered here to be a "sector" in the HL economy.

The accounts of rest of the world will be studied in this chapter. It should be emphasized that the accounting process for RW is not significantly different from that of the sectors into which the homeland economy was divided. This means that the divisions into the principal accounting statements and the principles for recording transactions presented in Chapters 2 and 3 are also valid for the RW sector.

8.2 Balance Statement for the Rest of the World

The balance statement for the rest of the world would include in concept (as does any other such statement) listings of all the assets and liabilities of all the countries of the world, with the exception of homeland. Net worth would be computed by the difference in these listings.

This consolidated statement would include as financial assets of RW only those that are liabilities of HL, and similarly, liabilities of RW include only the financial assets of HL.

In principle, there is no reason why the conceptual balance statement for RW described here could not be prepared. However, the statistical difficulties caused by lack of data or differences in the definitions used for the various components of the data available make its preparation impossible at this time.

In spite of the problems involved, however, any specific country, using the data available to it, can prepare the most important elements of a rest of the world statement. All the financial assets for RW are liabilities for HL as a whole, and, vice versa, all the financial assets for HL as a whole are liabilities for RW. As a result, using the information available in HL with respect to financial assets and liabilities with RW, it is possible to determine the value of the assets and liabilities of RW. Actually, the financial assets and liabilities of RW can be read from a consolidated statement of all the financial assets and liabilities in HL. When debits to a financial asset or liability in HL are not equal to its credits, the difference is a liability for RW if debits are larger than credits, or an asset for RW if credits are larger than debits.

These observations show how the value of financial assets and liabilities of RW can be obtained. The tangible assets of RW cannot be evaluated, and as a result, neither can net worth. However, these components of the balance statement of RW are not required in HL.

The balance statement for RW from the point of view of the United States is presented in Chapter 9, Table 9–1. The balance statement corresponding to the example for Chapter 8 appears later in this chapter, in Table 8–3.

8.3 Transactions of the Rest of the World

8.3.1 Description of the Principal Transactions

As already observed, rest of the world can be considered as a sector in the HL economy. This sector performs transactions similar to those of the other sectors, that is, it buys and sells goods and services, gives and receives credit both in cash and in goods or services, and pays and receives payment for these loans. These transactions are given special names when they refer to RW. The sales to RW or the purchases by RW are called *exports*, and the sales of RW to HL or the purchases from RW are called *imports*. Transactions including only financial assets and liabilities are frequently called *transactions in capital*.

A study of RW transactions does contain some points that may be confusing. First, an ordinary consumer or household does not usually have any transactions with RW. In most cases, commercial firms specialize in the import and/or export business, whether actually buying the goods from RW in order to sell them again in HL, or buying the goods in HL to export them to RW. In the analysis here it will be assumed that transactions are made directly between HL economic units and RW. This assumption does not change the nature of the transactions any more than the implicit assumption that households buy directly from industrial units, when in fact they buy from retailers.

A second confusing point is that HL and RW usually have different monetary units. This should not be a matter of concern if it is assumed that the rates of exchange are fixed, as is frequently the case. On the other hand, this is not the place for a discussion of how the rates of exchange are fixed. This topic is covered in the economic theory of international trade.

Frequently, payments made to RW or received from it are made through banks or similar financial institutions. In some cases, these operations are a function of the central bank alone. Again, this point will not be considered here, because it does not add anything essential to the transactions.

The list of the RW transactions considered in the example for Chapter 8 follows.

1. RW sells raw materials to HL Ind for $15.40: $10 paid by check, $5.40 credit (TR 2, 1, TR 3, 15, a).

2. RW Hh receive $1.50 interest from HL Ind paid by check: (TR 2, 7, b; TR 3, 15, b).

3. RW Hh receive $2.10 profits from HL Ind paid by check: (TR 2, 8, b; TR 3, 15, c).

4. RW purchases goods from HL Ind for $38.50: $35 paid by check, $3.50 credit (TR 2, 10, f; TR 3, 12, d).

5. RW sells to HL Hh:

    (a) Consumption goods worth $4.80: $4 paid by check, $0.80 credit (TR 1, 3, a; TR 3, 15, d);

    (b) Capital goods worth $1.70: paid by check (TR 1, 3, b; TR 3, 15, e);

    (c) Banking services for $1.10: paid by check (TR 1, 4, a; TR 3, 15, f).

6. RW sells capital goods:

    (a) To Ind for $3.20: $2.50 paid by check, $0.70 in credit (TR 2, 12; TR 3, 15, g);

    (b) To Bk for $1.10: paid increasing RW deposits (TR 3, 5).

7. RW pays $2.10 in wages to HL Hh: paid by check (TR 1, 8, c; TR 3, 11, h).

8. RW receives payments from HL Bk for:

    (a) Services provided for $0.30: paid increasing RW deposits (TR 3, 9, a);

    (b) Raw materials for $0.10: paid increasing RW deposits (TR 3, 9, b).

9. RW pays $0.40 to HL Bk for services provided: paid decreasing RW deposit account (TR 3, 10, b).

10. RW pay $2.10 in taxes to HL Gov: paid by check. (TR 3, 14, c; TR 4, 1, d).

11. RW sells goods worth $7.50 to HL Gov: $6 paid by check, $1.50 credit (TR 3, 15, h; TR 4, 5).

12. RW Bk sells services to HL Ind for $4.70: paid by check (TR 2, 13; TR 3, 15, i).
13. RW sells securities for $2.00 to HL Hh: paid by check (TR 1, 11, e; TR 3, 15, j).
14. RW buys shares for $8.00 from HL Ind: paid by check (TR 2, 18; TR 3, 12, g).
15. RW receives gold (a financial asset) valued at $10.00. Its deposit account is reduced (TR 3, 25).

8.3.2 Recording Rest of the World Transactions

In the examples in the previous chapters, several transactions were recorded. In all these transactions, the point of view of the sector being considered in that chapter was adopted. Basically, this means that the principles in Chapters 2 and 3 apply to the recording of the transactions. For example, if a firm obtains a loan from a bank, its liabilities and assets (cash or deposits) increase in the same quantity. In recording this transaction, the point of view of the firm is adopted and no attention is paid to the bank making the loan. The same transaction is later recorded from the point of view of the bank making the loan. In this case, no attention is paid to the firm's record of the transaction of the loan. The two records constitute a mirror reflection of each other.

These observations clarify the concept of recording a transaction from the point of view of an economic sector, which is useful when considering the accounts of RW. Here, transactions are recorded from the point of view of RW. This means, as stated before, that the accounting principles applied to each of the other sectors also apply to the RW sector. For even greater simplicity, it can be said that RW transactions are recorded as if RW were a firm within the HL economy, doing business with the other economic units within the HL economy.

The record of the transactions for the example for Chapter 8 is presented in Table 8–1.

8.4 The Rest of the World Transactions Statement

In principle, no modification is needed in the method used to prepare the transactions statement when this statement applies to RW. However, an important difference exists with respect to the classification of the accounts. The point is that, by definition, the cost of the goods sold by RW to HL is equal to the total value of the purchases by RW from HL. This should not come as a major surprise. The cost of the goods sold by, say, HL manufacturing is approximately equal to the purchases by manufacturing from the other sectors. The use that the manufacturing sector makes of its own production appears only as long as the accounts of the sector are not completely consolidated. When the accounts are consolidated, sales to itself cancel with part of the cost of goods in that sale. Only depreciation of the capital goods of manufacturing does not appear as a purchase. In the case of RW, the accounts of the sector are completely consolidated, that is, no attention is paid to the internal transactions of RW, and no distinction is made between purchases of consumption or capital goods. As a result, the cost of goods sold by RW to HL, that is, the imports of HL, must be exactly equal to the purchase by RW from HL.

These observations are illustrated in Table 8–2, presenting the RW transactions statement for the example for Chapter 8, and in Chapter 10, Table 10–3, for the U.S. economy.

8.5 Rest of the World Income and Product Statement

The procedure used to compute the income and product originating in transactions with the RW is the same as that used in all the other sectors. However, as has been the case with other sectors, new names are introduced for RW. In this case, in addition to the inconvenience of having to learn them, the new names are quite misleading. The statement of the income originating in the transactions with RW is called "foreign transactions accounts" in the United States accounts, and "external transactions accounts" in the United Nations system of accounts. These names are misleading because the statement does not refer to all the transactions of the sector, but only to those affecting the net worth of RW.

The balancing entry in the RW accounts corresponds to net income and savings in households, nondistributed profit in business, etc. It is called net foreign investment in some systems of accounts, and deficit or surplus in others. Observe that the balancing item can appear on either the debit or the credit side of the income and product statement. It is appears on the debit side, it means that total credits, that is, goods and services sold by RW to HL, are larger than debits, that is, goods and services bought by RW from HL. In other words, the sales of RW to HL are larger than its purchases from HL. This is called an unfavorable balance of trade for HL. When the balancing item appears on the credit side, the balance of trade is favorable to HL. Frequently, to add to the confusion, the balancing item is placed with a plus or minus sign on the debit side only.

In Table 8–3 the statement of the income and product originating in transactions with RW, computed from the data in the transactions state-

Table 8–1
Example for Chapter 8: Record of Rest of the World Transactions

Concept	Tangible Assets		Financial Assets		Liabilities		Net Worth	
	+Debit	−Credit	+Debit	−Credit	−Debit	+Credit	−Debit	+Credit
1. Sales Ind								15.4
Deposits Ind			10.0					
Accounts Receivable Ind			5.4					
2. Interest Received Ind								1.5
Deposits Ind			1.5					
3. Profits Received Ind								2.1
Deposits Ind			2.1					
4. Purchase Goods Ind							38.5	
Deposits Ind				35.0				
Accounts Payable Ind						3.5		
5a. Sales Hh								4.8
Deposits Hh			4.0					
Accounts Receivable Hh			0.8					
5b. Sales Hh								1.7
Deposits Hh			1.7					
5c. Sales Hh								1.1
Deposits Hh			1.1					
6a. Sales Ind								3.2
Deposits Ind			2.5					
Accounts Receivable Ind			0.7					
6b. Sales Bk Hh								1.1
Deposits Bk			1.1					

	Item	63.5	57.6	5.5	43.1	43.5
7.	Wages Hh Deposits Hh	2.1	2.1		2.1	
8a.	Services Bk Hh Deposits Bk	0.3				0.3
8b.	Raw Materials Hh Deposits Bk	0.1				0.1
9.	Services for Hh Deposits Bk	0.4	0.4		0.4	
10.	Tax Deposits Gov	2.1	2.1		2.1	
11.	Sales Gov Deposits Gov Accounts Receivable Gov	6.0 1.5				7.5
12.	Sales Ind Deposits Ind	4.7				4.7
13.	Sales Securities Deposits Hh	2.0		2.0		
14.	Shares Ind Deposits Ind	8.0	8.0			
15.	Gold Bk Deposits Bk	10.0	10.0			
	Total	63.5	57.6	5.5	43.1	43.5

Table 8–2
Example for Chapter 8: Transactions Statement, Rest of the World

	Debit	Credit
Financial Assets and Liabilities		
Deposits		
Hh	8.8	2.1
Ind	20.8	43.0
Bk	1.5	10.4
Gov	6.0	2.1
Other		
Hh	0.8	2.0
Ind	14.1	3.5
Bk	10.0	0.0
Gov	1.5	
Total Assets and Liabilities	63.5	63.1
Net Worth		
Sales Consumption and Intermediate		
Hh		5.9
Ind		20.1
Bk		0.4
Gov		7.5
Sales Capital		
Hh		1.7
Ind		3.2
Bk		1.1
Interest Ind		1.5
Profits Ind		2.1
Purchases Goods and Services		
Ind	38.5	
Bk	0.4	
Wages	2.1	
Tax	2.1	
Total Net Worth	43.1	43.5
Profit and Loss	0.4	
Total	106.6	106.6

ment in Table 8–2, is presented. The income and product statement for RW from the point of view of the United States appears in Chapter 10, at the bottom of Table 10–3.

Table 8–3

Example for Chapter 8: Summary of Accounting Process for Rest of the World

Accounts (1)	Initial Balance Debit (2)	Credit (3)	Transactions Statement Debit (4)	Credit (5)	Income and Product Debit (6)	Credit (7)	Final Balance Debit (8)	Credit (9)
Tangible Assets								
Financial Assets								
Gold			10.0				10.0	
Cash	3.5						3.5	
Deposits	29.2		37.1	57.6			8.7	
Accounts Receivable			8.4				8.4	
Securities	12.8						12.8	
Shares	22.2		8.0				30.2	
Gov Bonds	10.4						10.4	
Liabilities								
Accounts Payable				3.5				3.5
Securities		7.7		2.0				9.7
Shares		18.5						18.5
Net Worth		51.9						52.3
Shares				39.9		39.9		
Interests				1.5		1.5		
Profits				2.1		2.1		
Purchases of Goods and Services			38.9		38.9			
Wages			2.1		2.1			
Tax			2.1		2.1			
Income and Product						0.4		
Totals	78.1	78.1	106.6	106.6	43.5	43.5	84.0	84.0

8.6 Summary of the Rest of the World Accounting Process

The summary of the accounting process obtained from the example for Chapter 8 appears in Table 8–3.

8.7 Rest of the World Accounts and Balance of Payments

There are two equivalent ways of introducing the balance of payments.

1. If all transactions of the HL sectors are consolidated in one statement, that is, if the transaction statements for all the sectors are added

Table 8–4
Comparison of the Subdivisions in Balance of Payments and RW Accounts

RW Accounts	Balance of Payments
Tangible Assets	Capital Account
Financial Assets ⎫	Cash Account
Liabilities ⎭	
Net Worth	Current Account

together (all the quantities with their correct signs), the balance of payments for HL is obtained. In this aggregation, the transactions among HL sectors would cancel each other out because a debit in one HL sector is a credit in another HL sector or in RW, and vice versa. After all the quantities appearing in two or more HL sectors have been cancelled out, the balance of payments remains. This means that the balance of payments is the record of the transactions of the HL economy with the RW sector, from the point of view of HL.

2. This approach simply records the RW transactions from the point of view of HL. The equivalence between this approach and the first one is obvious.

From the preceding observations, it follows that the balance of payments is the "mirror reflection" of the RW transactions statement.

To complete the comparison between balance of payments and the RW account, the names of the main subdivisions of the balance of payments should be introduced. This is done in Table 8–4.

References

Mathews, R., *Accounting for Economists* (Chapter 18) (London: Angus and Robertson, 1969).

Powelson, J., *Economic Accounting (Chapters 16, 23) (New York: McGraw Hill, 1955).*

9

The National Balance Statement, National Wealth, and National Capital

9.1 Systematic Presentation of the Sectoral Balance Statements

The sectoral balance statements are systematic presentations of the assets, liabilities, and net worth of the different sectors. They are building blocks for the preparation of the national statement dealing with stocks.

The first step in the preparation of the national balance statement is the systematic presentation of all the sectoral balance statements. No separate classification for financial assets and liabilities can be maintained in this statement. This sytematic presentation of the sectoral balance statements for the United States of America appears in Table 9–1. Table 9–2 includes the systematic presentation of the balances in the examples for Chapters 3 to 8 as the example for Chapter 9.

This systematic table is useful because it shows how assets, liabilities, and net worth are distributed among the different economic sectors.

9.2 National Balance Statement and National Capital

The national balance statement is the consolidation, that is, the algebraic sum, of the sectoral balance statements. Several problems concerning this consolidation will now be discussed.

The basic balance equation in Chapter 2 is not modified. Some of the characteristics of its components in the consolidated statement follow from the consolidation process. By their nature, financial assets in one sector (including RW) appear as liabilities in other sectors, and vice versa. When the balance statements of all the sectors are consolidated, every financial asset that also appears as a liability is cancelled out. As a result, all that remains are tangible assets as debits, and national net worth as credits. All financial assets and liabilities cancel out. The remaining value of total tangible assets is called *national capital*. An estimate of the national capital of the United States in 1966 appears in Table 9–1, and one for the example for this chapter is found in Table 9–2.

It should be observed that if the tangible assets of the government do not include all public goods, such as roads and ports, the value of national capital underestimates the value of the stock of capital goods in the coun-

111

Table 9-1
United States: Balance Statements of Economic Sectors and Consolidated National Balance Statement, December 31, 1966 (10^9 1966 dollars)

Accounts	Hh		Business		Finance		Government		RW		Total	
	Debit	Credit	Debit	Credit	Debit	Credit	Debit	Credit	Debit	Credit	Debit	Credit
Tangible Assets[a]												
Consumer Durables	580.1										580.1	
Structures/Land/Other	228.4		784.5		13.9		230.0				1,429.4	
Equipment												
Inventories			172.6									
Financial Assets and Liabilities[a]												
Gold and Foreign Exchange					14.1	0.1	4.6	3.7	29.9	1.6	48.6	5.4
Treasure currency					6.2			4.0			6.2	4.0
Currency and Demand Deposit	88.6		47.2		13.5	185.7	18.7		2.8		170.9	185.7
Time and Saving Accounts	297.5		18.6		0.4	338.3	13.7		8.2		338.3	338.3
Life Insurance, Pension Fund Reserves	270.0					204.6		65.4			270.0	270.0
Consolidated Bank Items					27.9	27.9					27.9	27.9

Federal and State Securities	126.3		19.7		199.1		30.2	385.9	10.7		385.9	385.9
Corporate and Foreign Bonds	5.7	231.1		108.0	99.2	18.6	29.2		2.0	9.5	136.1	136.1
Corporate Stock	596.3		21.4	605.8[b]	91.7	34.3			12.6	60.5[b]	700.6	700.6[b]
Mortgages	9.9			87.0	289.3	1.3	20.0				319.3	319.3
Consumer Credit		94.8			73.3						94.8	94.8
Miscellaneous	18.2	28.8	232.7	289.1	167.3	100.6	53.0	15.4	18.2	88.8	489.3	522.7
Security Credit	1.6	9.0			15.8	8.5			0.2	0.1	17.6	17.6
Taxes Payable				20.6		1.8	22.4				22.4	22.4
Net Worth	1,858.9			186.2		90.0	−52.8		−75.9			2,006.7
Total	2,222.6	2,222.6	1,296.7	1,296.7	1,011.7	1,011.7	421.8	421.8	84.6	84.6	5,037.40	5,037.90

[a]Tangible assets estimate derived by using available data for 1958 (Goldsmith, *Studies in the National Balance Sheet of the United States*) and adding capital expenditures for years 1959 to 1966 inclusive (from *Flow of Funds Accounts 1945–1967*, FRB) and deducting capital consumption for households for years 1959 to 1966 inclusive (also from *Flow of Funds*). Financial assets and liabilities, *Federal Reserve Bulletin*, February, 1968, page A 65.10, Table 5.

[b]No value given in sources. The values presented in the table are valid only as arbitrary examples. The values are needed to compute the net worth of the sectors and national capital and wealth. As a result, these last two values are also arbitrary.

Table 9–2

Example for Chapter 9: Balance Statement of Economic Sectors and Consolidated National Balance Statement

Accounts	Households		Industry		Banks	
	Debit	Credit	Debit	Credit	Debit	Credit
Tangible Assets						
Consumer Durables	43.2					
Structures/Land	107.1		800.4		23.2	
Equipment			1,125.0		15.2	
Inventories Raw Materials			805.9		6.5	
Inventories Work in Process			15.3			
Inventories F. G.			18.2			
Financial Assets and Liabilities						
Gold and Foreign Exchange					16.9	
Cash	42.4		74.5			146.8
Deposits	95.6		115.2			308.9
Accounts Receivable and						
Payable	82.5	50.3	41.2	11.7	9.1	70.8
Securities	35.1			213.8	173.6	
Shares	2,315.9			1,513.5	258.6	64.7
Governments Bonds	95.8		15.3		93.5	
Net Worth		2,767.3		272.0		5.5
Totals	2,817.8	2,817.6	3,011.0	3,011.0	596.7	596.7

try. This is an important limitation, because the value of national capital is frequently used in economic models as one of the determinants of national production. If it is to be used for this purpose, national capital should also include the value of public capital goods.

9.3 National Wealth

National Wealth is obtained by adding the value

$$-1 \times (\text{RW financial assets} - \text{RW liabilities}),$$

that is, the value $-1 \times$ (net foreign balance) to the national capital.

The reason for this is that RW financial assets are the debts of HL to RW, and RW liabilities are the claims in favor of HL against RW. In consequence, a positive net foreign balance is the excess of debts of HL over claims in its favor. This excess should be subtracted from (that is, multiplied by -1 and added to) national capital. Likewise, a negative net foreign balance indicates the value owed by RW to HL. It should be added (that is, multiplied by -1 to make it positive and then added) to national capital to obtain national wealth.

Government		RW		Total		National Capital	
Debit	Credit	Debit	Credit	Debit	Credit	Debit	Credit
				43.2		43.2	
40.6				971.4		971.4	
60.3				1,300.5		1,300.5	
				812.4		812.4	
				15.3		15.3	
				18.2		18.2	
				16.9		16.9	
26.4		3.5		146.8	146.8		
68.9		29.2		308.9	308.9		
				132.8	132.8		
		12.8	7.7	221.5	221.5		
		22.2	18.5	2,596.7	2,596.7		
	215.0	10.4		215.0	215.0		
	−18.8		51.9		3,077.9		3,077.9
196.2	196.2	78.1	78.1	6,699.6	6,699.6	3,077.9	3,077.9

Again, if the tangible assets of government do not include all public tangible assets, national wealth would be understated.

From Table 9–1 it follows that U.S. national wealth in 1966 was 2082.6×10^9. The value from Table 9–2 is $3026.0.

9.4 Actual Estimation of Aggregated Balance Statements and of National Capital

In Chapters 3 to 8, sectoral balances were presented as a consolidation of the balances of the individual accounting units in each sector. In the same way, the national balance would be the consolidation of the individual balances of all the accounting units in an economy, and conceptually, that is the case.

In practice, few countries have attempted to prepare sectoral and national balances with an approach that could be described even remotely as a consolidation of individual balances. When this approach is used, a survey, whether by sample or complete enumeration, is used as a starting point. The information obtained in this way is combined with any other relevant information available, for example, that obtained from the department in charge of control of corporations. The evaluated information is integrated, using, in many cases, judgment and imagination to fill gaps and correct faulty data.

As already observed, times series of national capital are needed in many economic models used in the study of development and for policy and planning. Conceptually, the best way to obtain these data is from the national balance statements. However, as in many other cases, the urgency with which the information is needed does not always allow for a wait so that the appropriate method of obtaining it can be used. The most common method of estimating the value of national capital is to accumulate national investment for a period of, say, 20 years. The total value obtained in this way, in some cases corrected for depreciation, is used as the initial figure for capital.

The method described can be complemented with the following procedure. Assume that values Y_t, I_t, and L_t for output, investment, and labor employed at dates $t = 1, \ldots, T$ are available, and that the following constant returns to scale Cobb-Douglas production function holds:

$$Y_t = AR^t K_t^\alpha L_t^{(1-\alpha)} \tag{9.1}$$

where A = constant, R = rate of growth of disembodied technological change, K_t = capital at date t, and α = output/capital elasticity.

The problem is how to estimate the values of A, R, K, and α assuming that the values of Y_t, I_t, and L_t are known. For this, observe that

$$Y_j = AR^j \left[K_1\left(1 + \frac{N_j}{K_1}\right)\right]^\alpha L_j^{(1-\alpha)} \tag{9.2}$$

where

$$N_j = \sum_{h=2}^{j} I_h$$

For estimation purposes, the function in equation (9.2) must be linearized. In this case it takes the form

$$y_j = a + jr + \alpha k_1 + \alpha\ln\left(1 + \frac{N_j}{K_1}\right) + (1 - \alpha)\ell_j \tag{9.3}$$

where the expression in equation (9.3) can be further simplified by using the series expansion of logarithms to

$$y_j = (a + \alpha k_1) + jr + \alpha\frac{N_j}{K_1} + \frac{\alpha}{2}\left[\frac{N_j}{K_1}\right]^2 + (1-\alpha)\ell_j \tag{9.4}$$

where higher powers of N_j/K_1 are eliminated.

Regression analysis can be used to estimate the parameters of the following expression

$$y_j = b + rj + cN_j + d\ell_j \tag{9.5}$$

where b, c, d, and r are parameters to be estimated.

Once these values are obtained, a comparison of equation (9.4) and (9.5) shows that

$$\alpha = 1 - d$$

$$K_1 = \frac{1 - d}{c}$$

$$a = b - (1 - d)\ln\left(\frac{1 - d}{c}\right)$$

These equations can be improved to take into consideration reductions in the value of capital due to depreciation. When this is done, depreciation should affect both K_1 and I_j, $j = 2, \ldots, T$.

A limitation of this method is that N_j/K_1 should be less than or equal to 1, which limits the number of observations that can be considered. This limitation can be partially avoided by estimating the value of capital for some date in the middle of the period for which data are available, instead of K_1.

References

Goldsmith, R. W., Lipsey, R. E., and Mendelson, M., *Studies in the National Balance Sheet of the United States* (2 vols.) (Princeton: Princeton University Press, National Bureau of Economic Research, 1963).

Kendrick, J. W., *Economic Accounts and Their Uses* (Chapter 10) (New York: McGraw Hill, 1972).

Mathews, R., *Accounting for Economists* (Chapter 19) (London: Angus and Roberts, 1969).

10 The National Transactions Tables (NTT)

10.1 Basic Concepts

Two types of national transactions tables will be presented here. They will be called the detailed and nondetailed tables, denoted by DNTT and NDNTT. The basic ideas to be presented here are valid for both of them.

The national transactions tables are, with respect to the flows of real and financial assets and liabilities during an accounting period, what the systematic table of sectoral balance statements is with respect to the stocks of those variables at a fixed date. This means that the NTT are a systematic presentation of the transactions statements of all the sectors considered in an economy.

The classification problem already observed in the systematic table of sectoral balance statements reappears in the case of the national transactions table: the items appearing in one sector as financial assets (e.g., bank deposits for firms) are liabilities to other sectors (e.g., banks). Thus, the classification of assets and liabilities is eliminated. On the other hand, tangible assets and net worth accounts in one sector remain in the same classification for all other sectors. Therefore, the distinction between financial assets and liabilities has to be eliminated, while that of tangible assets and net worth can be maintained.

10.2 Detailed National Transactions Tables (DNTT)

An example of the DNTT appears in Table 10–1. Its main characteristic is that the accounts for each sector are subclassified in all the sectors; for instance, the cash account for Hh is subclassified in each of the five sectors, households, industry, etc. The same is true of all the other accounts and all the other sectors. The usefulness of this classification will be explained later.

Table 10–1, which can be subdivided into tangible assets (1 and 2), financial assets and liabilities (3 to 5), and net worth (6 to 10), is intended to emphasize the organization usually present in micro-accounting transactions statements. Later it will be seen that this basic organization is also needed when subdividing the NTT into partial macro-statements. On the other hand, to conserve space, only one aggregated account of nonmone-

119

Table 10–1
Example for Chapter 10: Detailed National Transactions Table

		Households		Industry		Banking		Government		Rest of the World		Total	
		Debit	Credit	Debit	Credit	Debit	Credit	Debit	Credit	Debit	Credit	Debit	Credit
1. Purchases of Capital, Fixed Investment	Hh	—	—	—	—	—	—	—	—	—	—	—	—
	Ind	21.1	—	77.6	—	5.9	—	—	—	—	—	104.6	—
	Bk	—	—	—	—	—	—	—	—	—	—	—	—
	Gov	—	—	—	—	—	—	—	—	—	—	—	—
	RW	1.7	—	3.2	—	1.1	—	—	—	—	—	6.0	—
	Total	22.8	—	80.8	—	7.0	—	—	—	—	—	110.6	—
2. Changes in Inventories and Capital Consumption	Hh	—	8.7	—	—	—	—	—	—	—	—	—	8.7
	Ind	—	—	15.0	53.7	—	—	—	—	—	—	15.0	53.7
	Bk	—	—	—	—	—	2.1	—	—	—	—	—	2.1
	Gov	—	—	—	—	—	—	—	—	—	—	—	—
	RW	—	—	—	—	—	—	—	—	—	—	—	—
	Total	—	8.7	15.0	53.7	—	2.1	—	—	—	—	15.0	64.5
3. Cash	Hh	—	—	70.0	81.6	27.0	28.0	40.2	14.7	—	—	137.2	124.3
	Ind	81.6	70.0	—	—	19.8	7.0	6.6	10.0	—	—	108.0	87.0
	Bk	28.0	27.0	7.0	19.8	—	—	1.9	—	—	—	36.9	46.8
	Gov	14.7	40.2	10.0	6.6	—	1.9	—	—	—	—	24.7	48.7
	RW	—	—	—	—	—	—	—	—	—	—	—	—
	Total	124.3	137.2	87.0	108.0	46.8	36.9	48.7	24.7	—	—	306.8	306.8
4. Deposits	Hh	—	—	453.0	416.2	40.0	50.4	50.0	113.0	8.8	2.1	551.8	581.7
	Ind	416.2	453.0	—	—	30.0	24.9	85.0	60.0	20.8	43.0	552.0	580.9
	Bk	50.4	40.0	24.9	30.0	—	—	4.0	1.2	1.5	10.4	80.8	81.6
	Gov	113.0	50.0	60.0	85.0	1.2	4.0	—	—	6.0	2.1	180.2	141.1
	RW	2.1	8.8	43.0	20.8	10.4	1.5	2.1	6.0	—	—	57.6	37.1
	Total	581.7	551.8	580.9	552.0	81.6	80.8	141.1	180.2	37.1	57.6	1,422.4	1,422.4
5. Financial Assets and Liabilities	Hh	—	—	44.3	55.0	6.1	13.0	—	15.0	0.8	2.0	51.2	85.0
	Ind	55.0	44.3	—	—	5.0	—	—	4.5	14.1	3.5	74.1	52.3
	Bk	13.0	6.1	—	5.0	—	—	—	—	10.0	—	23.0	11.1

Gov	15.0		4.5						1.5		21.0	
RW	2.0	0.8	3.5	14.1		10.0		1.5			5.5	26.4
Total	85.0	51.2	52.3	74.1	11.1	23.0		21.0	26.4	5.5	174.8	174.8
6. Purchases and Sales Consumption Goods and Services Households and Government												
Hh	481.2			481.2		10.1	74.5				555.7	497.2
Ind	10.1										11.3	
Bk				74.5		1.2	1.2					83.2
Gov	5.9								5.9			
RW							7.5		7.5		13.4	
Total	497.2			555.7		11.3	83.2		13.4		580.4	580.4
7. Purchases and Sales of Intermediate Goods and Services												
Hh		764.8	764.8		6.0						819.7	809.3
Ind		34.8				34.8						35.2
Bk			6.0		6.1	6.1					6.4	
Gov					0.4	0.4						
RW		20.1	38.5								38.9	20.5
Total		819.7	809.3		12.5	41.3					865.0	865.0
8. Sales of Capital Goods												
Hh		21.1									22.8	22.8
Ind		77.6									80.8	80.8
Bk		5.9									7.0	7.0
Gov												
RW												
Total		104.6									110.6	110.6
9. Wages, Profits, Rents Interests, Taxes												
Hh	487.8	487.8	28.4	75.2		3.6					646.0	75.2
Ind												583.0
Bk	28.4	91.6	5.9	91.6	2.1							34.3
Gov	127.7			5.9	2.1						174.8	127.7
RW	2.1	3.6		2.1							3.6	4.2
Total	646.0	583.0	34.3	174.8	4.2	3.6					824.4	824.4
10. Change in Inventories and Depreciation												
Hh	8.7										8.7	
Ind			53.7	15.0							53.7	15.0
Bk					2.1						2.1	
Gov												
RW												
Total	8.7		53.7	15.0	2.1						64.5	15.0
11. Total of Totals	1,394.9	1,394.9	2,272.4	2,272.4	189.3	189.3	400.7	400.7	106.6	106.6	4,363.9	4,363.9

tary financial assets and liabilities is presented. The subdivision into 6, 7, and 8 is frequently used in macro-economics, but would be impractical and difficult to implement for an accounting unit considered by itself. Account 9 aggregates all payments to households and government, while they are usually maintained apart in micro-accounting. Finally, 10 presents two accounts that usually appear in the net worth section of micro-transactions statements. In any case, it should be clear that the classification in accounts introduced here is arbitrary, and others could be used whenever practical applications suggest that they would be more useful.

10.3 The Nondetailed National Transactions Table (NDNTT)

The nondetailed national transactions table is a summary of the detailed table. It contains the total over sectors for each account. The nondetailed form of Table 10–1 uses only the total row for each account. Since the nondetailed form of the NTT corresponding to Table 10–1 will be used here, it is presented, at the risk of some repetition, in Table 10–2. The nondetailed NTT for the United States in 1966 appears in Table 10–3.

An important difference between Tables 10–1 and 10–2 on one hand and Table 10–3 on the other should be observed. In Tables 10–1 and 10–2 the totals of both debits and credits for each account are presented. In Table 10–3 only the consolidated value, that is, the value of the difference between debits and credits, is presented. The main reason for this is that the second type of information is much easier to obtain and it is sufficient for many uses. On the other hand, the complete information on debits and credits in Table 10–1 is needed for the preparation of the generalized equation of exchange.

10.4 Actual Estimation of the National Transactions Table

At present, perhaps Canada is the only country that prepares a yearly NTT. They can be prepared for any country having both sets of real or net worth national accounts, and financial national accounts. This has been done previously in the United States.

The observations to be made here on the actual estimation of the NTTs reflect the method used in the collection of net worth and financial national accounts in the countries that prepare these types of national statements. They also reflect the methods that should be used in the countries that at present do not prepare them.

As already observed, the NTT should be prepared by the aggregation

Table 10–2

Example for Chapter 10: Nondetailed Form of the National Transactions Table

	Household		Industry		Banking		Government		Rest of World		Total	
	Debit	Credit	Debit	Credit	Debit	Credit	Debit	Credit	Debit	Credit	Debit	Credit
Purchases of Capital	22.8	0.0	80.8	0.0	7.0	0.0	0.0	0.0	0.0	0.0	110.6	0.0
Changes Inventory Deposits	0.0	8.7	15.0	53.7	0.0	2.1	0.0	0.0	0.0	0.0	15.0	64.5
Cash	124.3	137.2	87.0	108.0	46.8	36.9	48.7	24.7	37.1	57.6	306.8	306.8
Deposits	581.7	551.8	580.9	552.0	81.6	80.8	141.1	180.2			1,422.4	1,422.4
Other Financial Assets and Liabilities	85.0	51.2	52.3	74.1	11.1	23.0	0.0	21.0	26.4	5.5	174.8	174.8
Final Consumption	497.2	0.0	0.0	555.7	0.0	11.3	83.2	0.0	0.0	13.4	580.4	580.4
Intermediate Purchases	0.0	0.0	819.7	809.3	6.4	35.2	0.0	0.0	38.9	20.5	865.0	865.0
Sales Capital Goods	0.0	0.0	0.0	104.6	0.0	0.0	0.0	0.0	0.0	6.0	0.0	110.6
Wages, Profits, Rents, Interests, Taxes	75.2	646.0	583.0	0.0	34.3	0.0	127.7	174.8	4.2	3.6	824.4	824.4
Changes Inventory Deposits	8.7	0.0	53.7	15.0	0.0	0.0	0.0	0.0	0.0	0.0	64.5	15.0
Totals	1,394.9	1,394.9	2,272.4	2,272.4	189.3	189.3	400.7	400.7	106.6	106.6	4,363.9	4,363.9

Table 10–3
National Transactions Table for the United States
(1966 data in 10⁹ dollars)

Source	(1)	Households Debit Uses (2)	Households Credit Sources (3)	Industries Debit Uses (4)	Industries Credit Sources (5)
	Tangible Assets				
F1,7	Residential Construction	18.4		6.0	
F1, 8	Plant and Equipment	4.4		74.8	
F1, 2–4,9 P1, 22	Capital Consumption		8.7		53.7
F1, 9	Inventory Change			13.4	
	Financial Assets and Liabilities				
F1, 13	Gold and Official US Foreign Exchange				
F1, 14	Treasure Currency				
F1, 15	Currency and Demand Deposits	1.9		0.7	
F1, 19	Time and Savings Accounts	19.2			0.7
F1, 22,23	Private Life Insurance and Pension Fund Reserve	11.6			
F1, 24	Consolidated Bank Items				
F1, 26,27	Government Securities	10.1		0.8	1.2
F1, 28, 29	Corporate and Foreign Stocks and Bonds	1.2	0.4		11.4
F1, 30, 31	Mortgages		12.7		7.5
F1, 32	Consumer Credit		6.9	1.4	
F1, 33	Bank Loans not elsewhere classified	0.1			9.9
F1, 34	Other Loans		1.8	2.3	4.8
F1, 37	Security Credit to Broker and Dealers	0.2			
F1, 41	Trade Credit		0.1	10.8	9.1
F1, 42	Equity in Noncorporate Business		7.4	7.4	
F1, 43	Miscellaneous Financial	1.2	0.4	5.7	6.6
	Total Assets and Liabilities	68.3	38.4	123.3	104.9
	Net Worth				
P1, 24	Personal Consumption Expenditures	465.9	8.7		441.1
P2, 4	Interest Paid by Consumers to Consumers	12.4	12.4		

Finance		Government		Rest of World		Total	
Debit Uses (6)	Credit Sources (7)	Debit Uses (8)	Credit Sources (9)	Debit Uses (10)	Credit Sources (11)	Debit Uses (12)	Credit Sources (13)
						24.4	
1.0						80.2	
	1.1						63.5
						13.4	
	0.3		0.2	0.6		0.6	0.5
0.7			0.9			0.7	0.9
0.4	2.6	0.8	0.1		0.3	3.8	3.0
	20.6	1.3		0.8		21.3	21.3
	12.8					11.6	12.8
2.3	2.3					2.3	2.3
4.3		1.0	12.3		2.6	16.2	16.1
10.4	4.7	4.4		0.9	0.4	16.9	16.9
16.7		4.1				20.8	20.2
5.5						6.9	6.9
9.6				0.2		9.9	9.9
5.9	4.3	4.6		0.3	1.2	13.1	12.1
0.4	0.6					0.6	0.6
0.2		1.2	0.8			12.2	10.0
						7.4	7.4
2.3	8.1	0.8		4.2	4.1	14.2	19.2
59.7	57.4	18.2	14.3	7.0	8.6	276.5	223.6
	10.8				5.3	465.9	465.9
						12.4	12.4

Table 10–3 (cont.)

Source	(1)	Households		Industries	
		Debit Uses (2)	Credit Sources (3)	Debit Uses (4)	Credit Sources (5)
P1, 17 P2, 14 P(1, 14), 8, 26	Personal Interest Income	9.1	39.1	29.3	
P1, 14–(1,14), 13, 31	Dividends		21.5	20.1	
P1, 9	Rental Income of Persons		19.4	19.4	
P(1, 13)	Wages, Salaries and Other Labor Paid by Government		71.6		
	Wages, Salaries and Other Labor Paid by Private Sector		343.8	327.7	
P1, 6 P2, 19	Contributions to Social Insurance	17.9		14.7	
P1, 8	Proprietors Income		59.3	59.3	
P1, 19 P2, 18	Transfer Payments to Nationals		43.9	2.7	
P1, 38	Government Purchases of Goods and Services				72.3
P1, 21 P3, 10, 11, 12	Subsidies less amount surplus of Gov Enterprises				2.2
P1, 12, 22, 11 P2, 1	Tax Payments and Receipts	75.2		91.6	
	Intermediate Goods and Services				
	Industries			764.8	764.8
	Financial			12.6	6.0
	Rest of the World			27.0	38.5
P1, 29	Gross Private Domestic Investment				104.6
P1, 34	Change in Inventories				13.4
P1, 22	Capital Consumption Allowance	8.7		53.7	
P1, 16	Inventory Evaluation Adjustment				1.6
P2, 5 P3, 4	Transfer Payments to Foreigners	0.6			
	Totals	658.1	658.1	1,546.2	1,549.4
	Totals only Net Worth's Debits, Credits	589.8	619.7	1,422.9	1,499.5
P2, 1—	Personal Savings	29.9			

Finance		Government		Rest of World		Total	
Debit Uses (6)	Credit Sources (7)	Debit Uses (8)	Credit Sources (9)	Debit Uses (10)	Credit Sources (11)	Debit Uses (12)	Credit Sources (13)
	9.1	9.9				48.3	48.2
1.4						21.5	21.5
						19.4	19.4
		71.6				71.6	71.6
14.0				2.1		343.8	343.8
0.6		5.0	38.2			38.2	38.2
						59.3	59.3
		41.2				43.9	43.9
	0.2	77.7			5.2	77.7	77.7
		2.2				2.2	2.2
5.9			174.8	2.1		174.8	174.8
6.0	12.6			38.5	27.0	809.3	804.4
6.1	6.1			0.4	0.4	19.1	12.5
0.4	0.4					27.4	38.9
							104.6
							13.4
1.1						63.5	
							1.6
		2.3			2.9	2.9	2.9
95.2	96.6	228.1	227.3	50.1	49.4	2,577.7	2,580.8
35.5	39.2	209.9	213.0	43.1	40.8		

128

Table 10–3 (cont.)

		Households		Industries	
		Debit Uses	Credit Sources	Debit Uses	Credit Sources
Source	(1)	(2)	(3)	(4)	(5)
P1, 15— P(1, 14)19,32	Undistributed Profits			21.6	
P3, 7	Government Surplus or Deficit				
P4, 5	Net Foreign Investment				
	Total Net Worth	619.7	619.7	1,444.5	1,449.5

Notes to Table 10–3: See Appendix to this chapter.

and consolidation of the transactions statements of all the accounting units in a country. This is a formidable task, but it is simplified by the following facts:

1. In most countries, the transactions for RW are obtained as a by-product of the customs controls on exports and imports. Actually, this type of statement (or its reflection, the balance of payments) was commonly used before any other form of sectoral transactions statement became available.

2. The government transactions statement is obtained as a by-product of fiscal controls on government receipts and expenditures. Most countries also have some statement on actual versus budgeted receipts and expenditures that can be used as a starting point for the preparation of the government transactions statement.

The main limitation of the information just given is that it refers exclusively to the central government. In principle, regional and local governments should also keep detailed records of their receipts and expenditures. Frequently, however, this is not done. Even if they could do so, in many cases there is no central office to collect and systematize all the information. Under these circumstances a department in charge of the preparation of the NTT should collect by sample or complete enumeration surveys the data for the regional and local governments.

3. Most banks, out of necessity, maintain high-quality accounts. In addition, most countries have somewhat centralized decision making in monetary policies and centralized control of the banking and financial institutions. The central financial and monetary authorities frequently prepare transactions statements for themselves, the commercial banks, and other financial institutions. These statements, although prepared as a

Finance		Government		Rest of World		Total	
Debit Uses (6)	Credit Sources (7)	Debit Uses (8)	Credit Sources (9)	Debit Uses (10)	Credit Sources (11)	Debit Uses (12)	Credit Sources (13)
3.7							
		3.1					
					2.3		
39.2	39.2	213.0	213.0	43.1	43.1		

guide for monetary and financial policies, satisfy the sectoral data requirements for the NTT.

4. According to these observations, sectoral transactions statements could be prepared for the three sectors considered, even if no NTT were evaluated. Unfortunately, this is not the case for households and industry. The only action open to a department in charge of the preparation of an NTT is to directly collect information on the transactions statements of all the individual units in these sectors, and, by consolidating them, to prepare the sectoral transactions statement. Detailed investigations are usually made only about every 10 years. In the intervening years, the results from the detailed investigation are updated, using (a) the characteristic of the NTT that the totals of debits in a row should be, in most cases, equal to the total of credits in the same row; (b) information obtained for tax purposes; and (c) whatever other information is available on production trends.

As observed here, the NTT is the parent statement of all other macro-accounting statements. As a result, the observations on the estimation of the NTT are valid for all other macro-statements as well. For this reason, the question of estimation of macro-statements will be mentioned again only when some details not previously discussed need to be presented.

10.5 Some Properties of the National Transactions Tables

Formally, the NTT can be described as a set of debit-credit vectors, one pair for each of the sectors considered in the economy. These vectors have the form

Debit	Credit
T_i	
D_{1i}	C_{1i}
D_{2i}	C_{2i}
	I_i
$D._i$	$C._i$

where the i subscript denotes sector, T_i = net tangible assets, D_{hi}, C_{hi} = debit and credit vectors, $h = 1$ for financial assets and liabilities, $h = 2$ for net worth accounts; I_i = investment; and

$$D._i = \sum_i D_{hi} + T_i$$

$$C._i = \sum_i C_{hi} + I_i$$

The NTT has the following properties:

1. The totals of debits and credits in the accounts of any sector are equal. This is a consequence of the fact that debit and credit columns for any one sector are simply the transactions statement of that sector. In the notation here, this can be expressed by $D._i = C._i$ for all i.

2. For the nondetailed NTT it is true that

$$\sum_i D_{hi} = \sum_i C_{hi}$$

that is, the row totals of debits are equal to the row totals of credits. This is because each transaction is recorded by pairs of accounting units in such a way that a debit for one is a credit for the other, and vice versa.

3. From these observations, it follows that

$$\sum_i T_i = \sum_i I_i$$

It is possible to derive a table of symmetric debit-credit matrices from the DNTT. That obtained from Table 10–1 appears in Table 10–4. The method used to obtain it is explained here.

Ten debit-credit matrices are presented in the NTT in Table 10–1. Each of these matrices deals with one particular tangible asset, financial assets and liabilities, or net worth accounts. Any one of these matrices is symmetric when a quantity that appears as a debit for one sector appears as a credit for another sector, and vice versa. It is always possible to pass from the NTT involving all accounting sectors to a set of symmetric debit-credit matrices. To obtain this result, the following steps are required:

1. Transactions involving only one sector usually refer to changes in inventories or to depreciation (matrices 2 and 10 in Table 10–1). To form the symmetric debit-credit matrix in this case, the matrices in the NTT dealing with those accounts in tangible assets and in net worth should be combined (matrices 6 and 7 in Table 10–4.)

2. Most of the transactions involving two units originate symmetric debit-credit matrices. This is so because when two units are involved, a transaction implies exchange, in which each unit gives and receives something. What is given by one unit is received by the other, that is, what is credit for the giving unit is debit for the receiving one, and vice versa. In addition, the items exchanged are classified in the same accounts.

The treatment of purchases of capital goods and their sale is an exception to this observation. As a consequence, matrices 1 and 8 are not symmetric in the NTT in Table 10–1. The symmetric matrix 5 in Table 10–4 is obtained by combining them.

An important observation is that if X_D denotes a matrix formed with the debit columns of a symmetric debit-credit matrix, and X_C denotes the matrix formed with the credit columns of the same symmetric debit-credit matrix, then

$$X_D' = X_C$$

where the prime symbol denotes transposition. This shows that either X_D or X_C contain the same information that the complete debit-credit matrix used as its starting point.

At this point it can be mentioned that it is possible to use the method to be presented in Chapter 12, Section 12.2.3 for the analysis of the table of symmetric debit-credit matrices. To avoid repetition, the details of the method will not be described here.

10.6 The National Transactions Table as the Basis for All the Statements of National Accounts

The importance of the NTT is that it is the basis for all the other statements of the national accounts. In Chapter 11 the derivation of the generalized equation of exchange (GEE) from the NTT will be described. The main purpose of this section is to explain how the NTT is subdivided in order to consider the partial national accounting statements.

Two types of partial statements will be defined in the following chapters: those dealing only with the financial aspects and those dealing with the real or net worth aspects of an economy. The only component of the first group is the flow of funds statement (FFS), while the second group includes input-output (IOS) and income and product (IPS) accounts.

Table 10–4
Example for Chapter 10: Debit-Credit Matrices Derived from Table 10–1

		Households		Industry		Banking		Government		Rest of the World		Total	
		Debit	Credit	Debit	Credit	Debit	Credit	Debit	Credit	Debit	Credit	Debit	Credit
1. Cash	Hh	—	—	70.0	81.6	27.0	28.0	40.2	14.7	—	—	137.2	124.3
	Ind	81.6	70.0	—	—	19.8	7.0	6.6	10.0	—	—	108.0	87.0
	Bk	28.0	27.0	7.0	19.8	—	—	1.9	—	—	—	36.9	46.8
	Gov	14.7	40.2	10.0	6.6	—	1.9	—	—	—	—	24.7	48.7
	RW	—	—	—	—	—	—	—	—	—	—	—	—
	Total	124.3	137.2	87.0	108.0	46.8	36.9	48.7	24.7	—	—	306.8	306.8
2. Deposits	Hh	—	—	453.0	416.2	40.0	50.4	50.0	113.0	8.8	2.1	551.8	581.7
	Ind	416.2	453.0	—	—	30.0	24.9	85.0	60.0	20.8	43.0	552.0	580.9
	Bk	50.4	40.0	24.9	30.0	—	—	4.0	1.2	1.5	10.4	80.8	81.6
	Gov	113.0	50.0	60.0	85.0	1.2	4.0	—	—	6.0	2.1	180.2	141.1
	RW	2.1	8.8	43.0	20.8	10.4	1.5	2.1	6.0	—	—	57.5	37.1
	Total	581.7	551.8	580.0	552.0	81.6	80.8	141.1	180.2	37.1	57.6	1,422.4	1,422.4
3. Financial Assets and Liabilities	Hh	—	—	44.3	55.0	6.1	13.0	—	15.0	0.8	2.0	51.2	85.0
	Ind	55.0	44.3	—	—	5.0	—	—	5.0	14.1	3.5	74.1	52.3
	Bk	13.0	6.1	—	—	—	—	—	—	10.0	—	23.0	11.1
	Gov	15.0	—	4.5	5.0	—	—	—	—	1.5	—	21.0	—
	RW	2.9	0.8	3.5	14.1	—	10.0	—	1.5	—	—	5.5	26.4
	Total	85.0	51.2	52.5	74.1	11.1	23.0	—	21.0	26.4	5.5	174.8	174.8
4. Consumption of Goods and Services	Hh	—	—	481.2	487.8	28.4	10.1	127.7	75.2	2.1	5.9	646.0	572.4
	Ind	481.2	487.8	764.8	764.8	6.0	34.8	74.5	91.6	38.5	23.7	1,365.0	1,402.7
	Bk	10.1	28.4	34.8	6.0	—	—	1.2	5.9	0.4	0.4	52.6	46.8
	Gov	75.2	127.7	91.6	74.5	5.9	1.2	—	—	2.1	7.5	174.8	210.9
	RW	5.9	2.1	23.7	38.5	0.4	0.4	7.5	2.1	—	—	33.9	43.1
	Total	572.4	646.0	1,402.7	1,365.0	40.7	46.5	210.9	174.8	43.1	33.9	2,275.9	2,275.9

5. Investment

Hh	—	—	21.1	—	—	—	1.7	—	22.8
Ind	21.1	77.6	77.6	5.9	—	—	3.2	104.6	80.8
Bk	—	—	5.9	—	—	—	1.1	—	7.0
Gov	—	—	—	1.1	—	—	—	6.0	—
RW	1.7	3.2	—	—	—	—	—	—	—
Total	22.8	80.8	104.6	7.0	—	—	6.0	110.6	110.6

6. Change in Inventories

Hh	—	—	—	—	—	—	—	—	—
Ind	—	15.0	—	—	—	—	—	15.0	15.0
Bk	—	—	—	1.0	—	—	—	1.0	1.0
Gov	—	—	—	—	—	—	—	—	—
RW	—	—	—	—	—	—	—	—	—
Total	—	15.0	—	1.0	—	—	—	16.0	16.0

7. Depreciation

Hh	8.7	—	—	—	—	—	—	8.7	8.7
Ind	—	53.7	—	—	—	—	—	53.7	53.7
Bk	—	—	1.1	—	—	—	—	1.1	1.1
Gov	—	—	—	—	—	—	—	—	—
RW	—	—	—	—	—	—	—	—	—
Total	8.7	53.7	1.1	—	—	—	—	63.5	63.5

Table 10–5
Subdivision of the National Transactions Table into Financial and Real Parts

Accounts	NTT Debit	NTT Credit	Content Debit	Content Credit	Name
(1)	(2)	(3)	(4)	(5)	(6)
Gross Savings				S_{1i}	
Tangible Assets	T_i		T_i		
Financial Assets and Liabilities	D_{1i}	C_{1i}	D_{1i}	C_{1i}	Flow of Funds
Total Financial			D_{Fi}	C_{Fi}	
Net Worth Accounts	D_{2i}	C_{2i}	D_{2i}	C_{2i}	
Investment					IOT and Income
Additions to Net Worth		I_i		I_i	and Product Accounts
			S_{2i}		
Total Net Worth			D_{wi}	C_{wi}	
Total NTT	$D_{.i}$	$C_{.i}$			

To obtain these statements, the NTT is divided into upper and lower parts. This is summarized in Table 10–5, which represents the NTT and the corresponding partial statement for one sector of the economy.

The content of the NTT for any sector is summarized in columns (2) and (3) of Table 10–5. Columns (4) and (5) show that the FFS is made up of the upper part of the NTT, and the IOS and IPS are the lower part. In addition to the totals D_{hi} and C_{hi} for $h = F,W$, the quantities S_{hi}, $h = 1, 2$, have been introduced. The values S_{hi} are calculated in such a way that the equality $D_{hi} = C_{hi}$, $h = F,W$, is obtained. S_{1i} is given the title of gross savings for all i. In the case of the real statements, different titles are given to the S_{2i}, depending on the sector being considered. For example, personal savings is used for households, undistributed profits for industries, government surplus for government, and net foreign investment for rest of the world. It should be clear that the S_{2i} are the net additions to net worth introduced in the micro-income and product statements in Chapter 2.

It will be verified that

$$S_{1i} = S_{2i} \tag{10.1}$$

It follows from the equality between debits and credits of the partial statements that

$$T_i + D_{1i} = C_{1i} + S_{1i}$$

and that

$$D_{2i} + S_{2i} = C_{2i} + I_i$$

The total of these two equations can be written as

$$D_{.i} + S_{2i} = C_{.i} + S_{1i}$$

implying the equality being verified. The definition of the S_{hi} and the equality in equation (10.1) provide a basis for interpreting them as a consolidation of the real transactions of sector i for $h = 1$ and of the financial transactions for $h = 2$.

The quantity $F_i = S_{1i} - T_i$ in the FFS is called the financial investment of sector i, and plays an important role in the interpretation of that statement. This suggests the possibility of defining what can be called the real transactions statement (RTS), in which T_i and F_i are used instead of S_{2i}. Some possible uses of the RTS will be mentioned later.

Appendix 10A:
Notes to Table 10–3

Table 10–3 is obtained as follows:
1. The basic sources are:

   (a) Board of Governors of the Federal Reserve System, *Flow of Funds Accounts 1945–1967*, February, 1968 (F)

   (b) "US National Income and Product Accounts, 1963–1966," in US Dept. of Commerce, *Survey of Current Business*, July 1967 (P)

   (c) Leontieff, W., *Input-Output Economics* (Chapter 2) (Oxford University Press, 1966)

The numbers following F or P used to denote references (a) and (b) indicate the tables in these sources from which the information was taken. When a table has two numbers, they appear in parentheses after F or P.

The input-output table in reference (c) was consolidated in Table 10A–1. The uses of this table will be explained here.

2. The data in source (a) were used mainly for the evaluation of assets and liabilities. The modifications that also affected net worth will be explained later. The data in sources (b) and (c) were used mainly for the evaluation of net worth. To do this, the national income and product account was deconsolidated, first to allocate production obtained by households and government (see later treatment of personal consumption expenditures and of wages), and second, to allocate the residual between industrial or nonfinancial business, finance, and rest of the world. In this the intersectoral transactions must be taken into consideration. The allocation of the residual was done as follows: first, the debits to net worth for the financial sector were estimated from data in source (b), Table 1–14. The residual minus the financial debits gave the consolidated debits of industries and rest of the world. Second, the allocation between industries and rest of the world and the estimation of the intersectoral sales among the three sectors were made using information in reference (c). Further explanation of the estimation of the credits appears later in note 6.

3. Consumer durables are recorded as in the national income and product accounts, and not as in the flow of funds accounts. This means that in Table 10–3

   a. The value of consumer durables is excluded from tangible assets and included in personal consumption expenditures.

   b. Depreciation of consumer durables is eliminated from the accounts. (F4.9)

Table 10A–1
Consolidated Input-Output Table

Row No.		Industry	28 Finance	Total	38 Inventories	39 Exports	40 Government	41 Private Capital Form	42 Households	Total
	Industry	230.54	1.82	232.36	4.94	15.38	16.39	33.28	152.10	454.45
28	Finance	3.80	1.85	5.65	0.0	0.14	0.03	0.0	6.99	12.81
38	Inventories	4.41	0.0	4.41	0.0	0.0	0.0	0.0	0.0	4.43
39	Imports	6.79	0.10	6.89	0.0	0.0	1.31	0.0	1.32	9.52
40	Government	26.18	1.11	27.29	0.34	0.83	3.46	0.0	31.55	63.47
41	Capital Formation	0.0	0.0	0.0	0.0	0.0	0.0	0.0	0.0	0.0
42	Households	182.62	7.93	190.55	0.0	0.85	30.06	0.0	2.12	223.58
	Total	454.34	12.81	467.15	5.28	17.20	51.25	33.28	194.08	768.24

Source: W. Leontieff, *Input-Output Economics* (Chapter 2, pages 16–19) (Oxford University Press, 1966).

Table 10A–2
Step 1: Distribution of Total between Government and Nongovernment

(1)	Total (2)		Government (3)		Nongovernment (4)	
	Source	Value	Source	Value	Source	Value
Salaries	P1.3	394.6	P1.13	70.4	b	324.2
Other Labor Income	P1.7	20.8	a	1.2	b	19.6
Social Insurance	P1.6	20.3	F1,22,23	5.0	b	15.3
Total	P1.1	435.7	P1.13	76.6	b	359.1

[a]Estimated by difference within same column
[b]Difference, column (2) − column (3)

c. The appropriate part of depreciation of residential construction and plant equipment (value obtained from source (a) remains in household's capital consumption. It also appears as (i) production that households sold to themselves; (ii) depreciation in household's net worth; and (iii) its value is reduced from sales and depreciation of industries.

d. The distribution of the remaining personal consumption among imports, industries, and finance was done as follows: For imports the share of Hh to total imports in Table 10A–1 was maintained with respect to total imports from P4.2. Total national consumption was distributed between industries and finance in agreement with the proportion of household consumption in column 42, Table 10A–1. From the value obtained for finance, Hh depreciation was subtracted because the value obtained in this way seemed more acceptable.

4. Personal interest includes total interest (except interest paid by consumer to consumer) and not merely interest that is a "product" of industry and finance. This product of industry and finance, valued at 20.2 billion, appears in P1.17. The payments of 9.1 billion from industry to households and from households to finance are added to this. This value is estimated from Table P1.14, lines 8 and 26. Finally, general interest is added.

5. The estimation of wages, salaries, and contribution to social insurance was made in the two steps described in Tables 10A–2 and 10A–3.

6. Contributions to government social insurance are recorded as in the national income and product accounts, and not as in the flow of funds accounts, that is, these payments are treated as expenditures and not as

Table 10A–3
Step 2: Distribution of Nongovernment among Industry, Finance, and Rest of the World

	Nongovernment	Industry	Finance	Rest of the World
Salaries	324.2	309.2[a]	13.1[a]	1.9[a]
Other Labor Income	19.6	18.5	.9[a]	.2[a]
Social Insurance	15.3	14.7	.6[a]	.0[b]
Total	359.1	342.4[c]	14.6[c]	2.1[c]

[a]Estimated assuming that proportion in column (1) holds
[b]Assumed to be zero
[c]Estimated as described in note 2 using input-output matrix data

savings in source (a). They are excluded from line F1, 22, 23 and included in line P1, 6, P2, 19.

7. Government consumption from P1,38 was computed as follows: First, givernment wages from step 5 were deducted from total government consumption. Second, government imports were estimated using the proportion in row 39 of Table 10A–1 and the total from P4.2. Finally, the residual was distributed according to column 40, Table 10A–1.

8. Tax payments and receipts from P3, 10, 11, 12 were distributed as follows: Household tax reports were obtained from P2.1. Finance tax payments were obtained from P1.14 lines 3 plus 11 minus 21 and 29. The residual was distributed between industries and rest of the world in agreement with the proportion obtained from row 40 of Table 10A–1.

9. Industry, finance, and imports or exports were used to estimate intermediate goals and services. The first step was to obtain Table 10A–4 from Table 10A–1.

Next, total production for these sectors was computed for the sum of the total row: $454.34 + 12.81 + 17.20 = 484.35$ (Table 10A–1).

The quotient $484.35/(484.35-260.40)$ gave a relation of final uses to total production and was used to expand the total P1, last line, to obtain total production in 1966. By differences the intermediate production for 1966 was estimated to be 863.93. The proportion $863.93/260.40$ was used to expand the totals in Table 10A–4.

The quotients of the expanded values to the totals of each row and columns were used to expand the components of industry, finance, and imports. The results obtained with row expansion appear in parentheses following the original values in Table 10A–4. The results obtained with the column totals appear second.

The values obtained for industry and finance in Table 10A–4 are used

Table 10A–4
Industry, Finance, Export, Sum, and Expansion

	Industry	Finance	Export	Sum	Expansion
Industry	230.54	1.82	15.38	247.72	821.85
	(764.77)	(6.03)	(51.02)	(821.86)	
	(764.86)	(6.03)	(51.03)		
Finance	3.80	1.85	0.14	5.79	19.31
	(12.66)	(6.16)	(0.47)	(19.31)	
	(12.60)	(6.13)	(0.46)		
Imports	6.79	0.10	0.0	6.89	22.76
	(22.45)	(0.33)	(0.0)	(22.76)	
	(22.53)	(0.33)	(0.0)		
Sum	241.13	3.77	15.82	260.40	
	800.00	(12.50)	(51.43)		
Expansion	800.00	12.50	51.93		863.93

in Table 10–3. However, the results obtained for imports and exports are not consistent with the totals in P4, 1, 2, and the previously estimated rate of imports of household and government. For this reason the estimates in Table 10A–4 were replaced by the following ones: For exports the proportion between P4.1 and the total of column 39 in Table 10A–1 was used to expand the components of the same column. For imports the proportion between P4.2 and the total of row 39 was used to estimate the components of the same row. The results that are consistent with previous estimates of exports and imports are used in Table 10–3.

11

Macro-Accounting Statement Dealing with Real and Financial Aspects: The Generalized Equation of Exchange (GEE)

11.1 Introduction

In economic theory the equation of exchange is usually associated with the formulation Fisher gave to it and with the quantitative theory of money. In this case, the equation takes the form

$$VM = PQ \qquad (11.1)$$

where V = velocity of circulation, M = money supply, P = price index, and Q = quantity of goods index.

However, from a logical point of view, equation (11.1) cannot be the point of departure.

Instead, the starting point is the intuitive idea that the value of all goods, services, and claims sold is equal to that of the units of money used to pay for them. The next step, not satisfactorily completed up to the present time, must be to provide that intuitive idea with a more precise content. In order to do so, aggregated and disaggregated forms of the equation of exchange will be derived from the NTT. This procedure gives a solid micro-accounting basis to the equation of exchange and integrates it with macro-accounting.

The aggregated and disaggregated forms of the GEE to be obtained here logically come before, are independent of, and also are more general than any particular formulation or theory in which they are used, for example, those associated with equation (11.1). On the other hand, it is useful to mention the extent to which existing formulations of theories can be recast into the two forms of the GEE. It will also be shown that this is true of the standard Fisher's formulations. In the present case this means that the concept of velocity of circulation can be adapted to the GEE. It should be added, however, that if this were not the case, and if the derivation of the GEE to be presented here is correct, then Fisher's formulation would have to be modified.

11.2 The Generalized Equation of Exchange

11.2.1 Introduction

In this section the disaggregated and the aggregated generalized equations of exchange are derived from the NTT. The disaggregated GEE is presented first, because only this form of the equation has a clear link with the NTT. The aggregated GEE is derived from the disaggregated.

11.2.2 The Disaggregated Generalized Equation of Exchange

In Section 10.5 "mathematical" matrices were derived from the symmetric debit-credit matrices obtained from the DNTT. These matrices were presented in Table 10–4. They will be used to form the GEE.

To simplify, it will be assumed that all matrices dealing with money have been added together. The same assumption is made for all matrices dealing with deposits, with financial assets and liabilities, and with net worth. This assumption makes it possible to write the GEE in a compact form without affecting its generality. It can be discarded with the only additional complication that the GEE has to deal with a larger number of matrices.

With the assumption just presented, the GEE takes the form

$$M' + D' + R' = F + N \tag{11.2}$$

where M' = cash matrix, D' = deposits matrix, R' = residual matrix, F = financial matrix, and N = net worth matrix (as usual, the prime symbol means transposition).

With the exception of R', all the matrices in equation (11.2) are obtained from the NTT using the methods described in Section 10.5. The matrix R' is obtained by difference.

The GEE derived from the NTT in Table 10–1 and the symmetric matrices in Table 10–4 are presented in Table 11–1. A detailed interpretation of the GEE equation will be presented here. The M' matrix has as column j the credit $(-)$ side of the cash account of sector j (credit because M' is the transpose of the M matrix with debit columns). This means that all cash payments of sector j to the other sectors appear in matrix M', column j. All receipts (debits $+$) of sector i from the other sectors appear in row i.

Matrix D' has a similar interpretation. Column j is the credit $(-)$ side of the deposits account of sector j with the other sectors, d'_{ij} the payments of sector j to sector i by check.

In summary,

$$\sum_{j=1} (m'_{ij} + d'_{ij})$$

shows the payment received by sector i both in cash and by check.

Table 11–1
Example for Chapter 11: Generalized Exchange Equation (GEE)

M'

0.0	81.6	28.0	14.7	0.0
70.0	0.0	7.0	10.0	0.0
27.0	19.8	0.0	0.0	0.0
40.2	6.6	1.9	0.0	0.0
0.0	0.0	0.0	0.0	0.0

$+$

D'

0.0	416.2	50.4	113.0	2.1
453.0	0.0	24.9	60.0	43.0
40.0	30.0	0.0	1.2	10.4
50.0	85.0	4.0	0.0	2.1
8.8	20.8	1.5	6.0	0.0

$+$

R'

8.7	34.3	-43.9	0.0	0.8
34.3	911.1	-15.0	4.5	9.6
-43.9	-15.0	8.2	0.0	0.0
0.0	4.5	0.0	0.0	1.5
0.8	9.6	0.0	1.5	0.0

$=$

F

0.0	44.3	6.1	0.0	0.8
55.0	0.0	5.0	0.0	14.1
13.0	0.0	0.0	0.0	10.0
15.0	4.5	0.0	0.0	1.5
2.0	3.5	0.0	0.0	0.0

$+$

N_1

0.0	487.8	28.4	127.7	2.1
481.2	764.8	6.0	74.5	38.5
10.1	34.8	6.1	1.2	0.4
75.2	91.6	5.9	0.0	2.1
5.9	23.7	0.4	7.5	0.0

$+$

N_2

8.7	0.0	0.0	0.0	0.0
21.1	146.3	5.9	0.0	0.0
0.0	0.0	2.1	0.0	0.0
0.0	0.0	0.0	0.0	0.0
1.7	3.2	1.1	0.0	0.0

N_1 = consumption and intermediate goods and services; N_2 = capital goods, change in inventories, depreciation; $N = N_1 + N_2$ in equation (11.2).

The F matrix has as column j the debit column of sector j. This debit column is the total of debits to financial assets ($+$) and to financial liabilities ($-$). Debits to financial assets of sector j ($+$) denote loans that sector j makes to the other sectors. Debits to liabilities of sector j ($-$) denote reductions of the liabilities of sector j due to payments of debts. Both types of debits can be interpreted as purchases by sector j of financial documents from the other sectors. In summary, column j of matrix F is formed with the payments or transfers of money made by sector j to the other sectors in order to receive financial documents. Row i of matrix F denotes the money received by sector i in exchange for financial documents sold to the other sectors.

Matrix N has as column j the debits ($-$) appearing in the net worth account of sector j. These debits ($-$) are due to payments of wages, interest, profits, rent, purchases of goods and services, etc.; that is, column j shows the purposes of payments by sector j to the other sectors and the amounts paid. Row i shows why sector i received payments from the other sectors and the amounts paid. Row i shows why sector i received payments from the other sectors and the amounts received.

A summary of the right-hand side of the GEE shows that

$$\sum_{j=1} (f_{ij} + n_{ij})$$

is equal to payments received by sector i, classified by reason for the payment.

With the exception of matrix R', which we have not yet analyzed, row i of the left-hand side of the GEE is the total payment in cash or check received by sector i, while the same row on the left-hand side is the total value of sales of goods, services, and financial documents of sector i.

The existence of matrix R' shows that some transactions affect only one side of the GEE. These transactions will be described here, and it will be shown that R' is a symmetric matrix in the usual mathematical sense.

Deposits and withdrawals of cash from banks affect only matrices M' and D'. To study this in more detail, let b be the subscript for banks and t for some other sector. A withdrawal is included in the element $d'_{b,t}$ of D', since it is a credit in the deposit account of sector t. However, it is not included in $d'_{t,b}$ because a withdrawal is a debit in the bank account. The withdrawal also appears in $m'_{t,b}$ because it is a credit ($-$) in the cash account of the banks. It does not appear in column t of matrix M', because the cash received is a debit for sector t. In summary, a withdrawal appears in row b and column t and in row t and column b of $M' + D'$, and it does appear in $F + N$. It follows that a withdrawal appears in both $r'_{b,t}$ and $r'_{t,b}$, that is, matrix R' is symmetric with respect to withdrawals.

It can be similarly shown that deposits in cash appear in $m'_{b,t}$ as a credit ($-$) to the cash assets of sector t, and in $d'_{t,b}$ as a credit to the deposits liability of the banks, and, as a result, that R' is symmetric with respect to deposits.

Three types of transactions affect only the right-hand side of the GEE. The first type is a transaction in which a real good or service is exchanged for a financial asset. To study this, let us assume that sector s sells consumption or intermediate goods and services to sector t and receives a financial document in exchange. The consumption $n_{s,t}$ of sector t from sector s is a debit ($-$) for t and appears in row s of column t. It does not appear as a sale from s to t, that is, row t and column s, because it is a credit ($+$) for s. The financial asset that t uses to pay s for the purchase is a debit ($+$) to assets for s and a credit ($+$) to liabilities for t. As a result, it appears in $f_{t,s}$, that is, row t, column s of matrix F, but it does not appear in row s and column t of the same matrix. In summary, a transaction between s and t of the type just considered appears in elements (s,t) and (t,s) of matrix $F + N$, but it does not appear in matrix $M' + D'$. As a result, it will appear in elements (s,t) and (t,s) of matrix R'.

The second types of transactions affecting only the right-hand side of the GEE are those that represent an exchange of one financial asset for another. The fact that these transactions do not affect the symmetry of R' will not be verified here. This proof follows steps similar to those used earlier.

Internal transactions are the third type of transactions that affect only the right-hand side of the GEE. The use of inventories of raw materials, whether purchased or produced by the accounting unit, are an example of this type of transaction. They affect only the main diagonal of the N matrix, and as a result, appear only in the main diagonal of matrix R', and do not affect its symmetry.

So far, the validity of equation (11.2) has been established only when the subdivision of an economy into sectors is considered. It will be shown that it is also valid when an economy is aggregated in one sector.

11.2.3 The Aggregated Equation of Exchange

From a purely mathematical point of view, the aggregated equation follows from the product

$$(1)'M'(1) + (1)'D'(1) + (1)'R'(1) = (1)'F(1) + (1)'N(1)$$

where (1) is a column vector of ones with the appropriate dimensions. The results obtained by using the data in Table 11–1 in this equation appear in Table 11–2.

To justify the separate columns for debit and credit in Table 11–2, and

Table 11–2
Example for Chapter 11: Aggregated Form of the GEE

	Debit	Credit
Money Payments	306.8	306.8
Check Payments	1422.4	1422.4
Residual	911.6	911.6
Total	2640.8	2640.8
Financial Assets and Liabilities	174.8	174.8
Consumption and Intermediate Goods and Services	2275.9	2275.9
Capital Goods, Change in Inventories, Depreciation	190.1	190.1
Total	2640.8	2640.8

to show the economic meaning of the results, it is necessary to return to the symmetric debit-credit matrices used to derive the GEE. For this, the R' matrix must be transformed into a debit-credit matrix. Since the R' matrix is symmetric, the debit-credit matrix corresponding to it has the same values in the debit and in the credit columns for each sector. The debit-credit matrix derived from R' could differ from accounting practice in that it might have some negative entries.

To obtain the aggregated GEE, the debit columns and the credit columns of the debit-credit matrices are added to obtain totals for each row. The debit totals and the credit totals by row are added to obtain the totals by account. The totals obtained appear in Table 11–2. As could be expected, the debits for each account are equal to the credits for the same account. The aggregated GEE is either one of the two columns of Table 11–2.

It should be observed that this method of aggregation eliminates all possibility of the double counting which would occur if a purchase of goods, services, or financial assets were counted once in the sector making the purchase and once in the sector making the sale, and both evaluations added to obtain the aggregated GEE. The left-hand side of Table 11–2 is the total of debits only, that is, it includes only purchases without sales. The right-hand side includes only credits, that is, payments for purchases. Any possibility of duplication is thus avoided.

11.3 Velocity of Circulation in the GEE

As observed in Section 11.1, the equation of exchange is usually associated with the formulation in equation (11.1). However, as already indicated, from a logical point of view the first step should be that accomplished in

Section 11.2. Only after the intuitive idea that money payments are equal to the value of goods and services transacted is given an accounting basis is it possible to proceed to an analysis of the relationship.

On the other hand, it is important to discover to what extent the GEE can be expressed in the form in equation (11.1). This is particularly true of the concept of velocity of circulation, because this concept seems to have a strong relationship to the facts, and is useful in the study of monetary processes.

It should be clear that the standard concept of velocity of circulation, that is,

$$V = \frac{\text{total payments in the economy}}{\text{stock of money in the economy}} \qquad (11.3)$$

can be applied without modification to the aggregated form of the GEE. As a result, only the extension of the concept to the disaggregated form needs to be discussed.

The presentation here will be restricted to the cash velocity of circulation; however, it should be clear that the basic ideas, properly modified, are also valid in the case of deposits.

For this, and with respect to matrix M', the row totals

$$m._{j} = \sum_{i} m'_{ij}$$

the column totals

$$m_{i.} = \sum_{j} m'_{ij}$$

and the quotients of a component to the total of its column

$$f_{ij} = m'_{ij}/m._{j}$$

will be considered. These elements are related by the identity

$$[f][m._{j}]' = [m_{i.}]' \qquad (11.4)$$

This identity establishes a relationship between payments and receipts of the different sectors.

To define the currency velocity of circulation for a nonbanking sector, to be denoted by j, its total payments must be related to the stock of currency it holds at a date taken as a reference. These sectoral stocks are accounted for as debits in the balance statement of the sector. They will be denoted here by S_{j}.

A problem arises when the banking sector is considered, because in its consolidated balance statement only the cash held by the nonbank sectors of the economy appear as a credit. This is so despite the fact that, obviously, the banking system holds cash to be used for transactions.

Table 11–3
Example for Chapter 11: Total Velocities of Cash Circulation for the Economic Sector

Sector	Total Payments from Table 11–1	Stocks of Cash for Table 9–2	Total Velocity of Circulation
Households	137.2	42.4	3.24
Industry	108.0	74.5	1.45
Banks	36.9	3.6[a]	10.25
Government	24.7	26.4	0.94
Rest of the World	0.0	3.5	0.0
Total	306.8	150.4	2.04

[a]See observations in text.

This problem is only partially solved if the banking system is deconsolidated into central and commercial banks. In this case the commercial banks have cash assets and, as a result, the problem is solved for them. However, the problem remains for the central bank.

A simple solution, but one without accounting basis, is to estimate by direct investigation the amount of cash that the banking system holds for transactions. In the examples to be presented here it will be assumed that this solution has been used. A different type of solution based on mathematical considerations will be described later.

It is useful to observe that if banks open deposit accounts in other banks, as is usually the case, the problem just discussed does not appear for the definition of velocity of demand deposits.

Once the S_j are evaluated for all the sectors, the velocity of circulation of sector j with respect to its total payments can be defined by the proportion

$$v_j = m_{.j}/S_j \qquad (11.5)$$

The values obtained from Tables 9–2 and 11–1 appear in Table 11–3.

In addition, the "partial" velocities of circulation for payments from one sector to another can be equated, by definition, with the components of the matrix

$$[fv] = [f_{ij}v_j]$$

obtained by multiplying the total sector velocites v_j by the components of column j of the matrix $[f]$ defined earler.

To justify this definition, one can use the fact that

$$[fv][\hat{S}_j]$$

where $[\hat{S}_j]$ is a diagonal matrix with the sectoral stocks S_j in the main diagonal, has as components those of the matrix $[M]'$, that is, the payments of sector j to sector i, and

$$[fv][S_j] = [m_{i.}]'$$

Digressing from the main purpose of this section, some observations with respect to the equilibrium values of the velocities of circulation defined earlier, will be made here.

The equilibrium value of payments and receipts corresponding to a matrix $[f]$ would clearly satisfy the condition $[m_{.j}]' = [m'_{i.}] = [m]$. This means that the system in equation (11.4) has an infinite number of solutions of the form $a[m^*]$ where a is a number, and $[m^*]$ is a particular column vector satisfying equation (11.4) and the equality between payments and receipts.

From an economic point of view it is meaningful to determine $[m^*]$, using as a side constraint the equality

$$(1)[m^*] = P$$

where (1) is a row vector with all components equal to 1 and P is the value of total payments in the economy. With this, the components of $[m^*]$ can be interpreted as the equilibrium payments and receipts of the different sectors.

Also under conditions of equilibrium, and if currency is used only for transaction purposes, the currency paid must be equal to the currency received. This means that in equilibrium, the stock of currency used for transaction purposes only also satisfies the equation

$$[f][S^*] = [S^*] \qquad (11.6)$$

where the meaning of $[S^*]$ should be clear.

It should be observed that none of the limitations of the observed values of S_j defined here affect the equilibrium stock of currency in the banking system, obtained as one of the components of the vector $[S^*]$ defined in equation (11.6). As a result, the values of this component could be used in equation (11.5).

From the fact that the vectors $[m^*]$ and $[S^*]$ satisfy the equilibrium form of equation (11.4), it follows that

$$[S^*] = a[m^*]$$

This means that all the sectoral velocities have a common value $v = 1/a$, and that as a consequence

$$v = \frac{\text{equilibrium payments of sector } i}{\text{equilibrium stocks of cash sector } i}$$

$$= \frac{\text{total payments in the economy}}{\text{stock of cash in the economy}}$$

It should be emphasized that these conditions do not hold if currency is used for nontransaction purposes.

12

Macro-Accounting Statement Dealing with Financial Aspects Only: The Flow of Funds Statement (FFS)

12.1 Derivation of the Flow of Funds Statement from the National Transactions Table

The FFS is obtained from the upper part of the nondetailed form of the NTT, that is, it includes tangible assets along with financial assets and liabilities. The level of disaggregation of these accounts varies in different tables.

In addition to the elements of the NTT just mentioned, the FFS includes gross savings, financial investment, and financial uses and sources. The form in which these elements appears in the FFS can be seen in Table 12–1 (derived from Table 10–1) and in Table 12–2, which contains an outline in symbols of the statement.

The definitions and properties of the elements of the FFS that do not appear in the NTT will be described here in detail.

Clearly, the total of all the debits differs from that of all the credits for each of the accounting units in the partial table obtained from the upper part of the NTT, that is, with the notation of Table 12–2, $T_i + D_{1i} + D_{2i} \neq C_{1i} + C_{2i}$, $i = 1,5$. It was observed in Section 10.5 that to obtain the balance of the debits and credits for each sector of the economy (that is, to obtain $D_{.i} = C_{.i}$, $i = 1,5$), a new element called gross savings is introduced in the statement. As also observed in Section 10.5, the gross savings (S_i, $i = 1,5$) are equal to the additions to net worth for each of the accounting units in the economy.

A property of gross savings for the economy as a whole, that is,

$$S. = \sum_{i=1}^{5} S_i$$

is that it is equal to tangible investment

$$T. = \sum_{i=1}^{5} T_i$$

This follows from the fact that $D_j. = C_j.$, $j=1,2$, as already observed in the NTT, and that $D = c$ since $d\ D = \Sigma D_{.i}$ and $C = \Sigma C_{.i}$.

Financial investment is defined to be

$$F_i = S_i - T_i \qquad i = 1,5$$

153

Table 12–1
Example for Chapter 12: National Flow of Funds Statement (FFS)

	Households		Industry		Banking		Government		Rest of the World		Total	
	Debit Uses	Credit Sources	Debit Uses	Credit Sources	Debit Uses	Credit Sources	Debit Uses	Credit Sources	Debit Uses	Credit Sources	Debit Uses	Credit Sources
Savings		64.9		28.2		3.7		-36.1		0.4		61.1
Depreciation		8.7		53.7		1.1[b]						63.5
Tangible Investment	22.8		95.8		6.0[a]						124.6	
Financial Investment	50.8		-13.9		-1.2		-36.1		0.4			
Financial Uses	791.0		720.2		139.5		189.8		63.5			
Financial Sources		740.2		734.1		140.7		225.9		63.1		
Cash	124.3	137.2	87.0	108.0	46.8	36.9	48.7	24.7			306.8	306.8
Deposits	581.7	551.8	580.9	552.0	81.6	80.8	141.1	180.2	37.1	57.6	1422.4	1422.4
Other Financial	85.0	51.2	52.3	74.1	11.1	23.0	0.0	21.0	26.4	5.5	174.8	174.8
Accounts Payable and Receivable	0.0	36.2	42.3	11.1	6.1	0.0	0.0	6.0	8.4	3.5	56.8	56.8
Securities	47.0	10.0	10.0	40.0	0.0	5.0	0.0	0.0	0.0	2.0	57.0	57.0
Shares	18.0	0.0	0.0	23.0	0.0	3.0	0.0	0.0	8.0	0.0	26.0	26.0
Gov Bonds	20.0	5.0	0.0	0.0	5.0	5.0	0.0	15.0	0.0	0.0	25.0	25.0
Financial Gold	0.0	0.0	0.0	0.0	0.0	10.0	0.0	0.0	10.0	0.0	10.0	10.0
Total	813.8	813.8	816.0	816.0	145.5	145.5	189.8	189.8	63.5	63.5	2028.6	2028.6

[a]Total investment minus reduction of inventories
[b]Capital consumption, reduction of inventories

Table 12–2
Outline of an FFS

	Households		Industry		Banking		Government		Rest of the World		Total	
	Debit Uses	Credit Sources	Debit Uses	Credit Sources	Debit Uses	Credit Sources	Debit Uses	Credit Sources	Debit Uses	Credit Sources	Debit Uses	Credit Sources
1. Gross Savings		S_1		S_2		S_3		S_4		S_5		$S_{.}$
2. Tangible Investment	T_1		T_2		T_3		T_4		T_5		$T_{.}$	
3. Financial Investment	F_1		F_2		F_3		F_4		F_5		$F_{.}$	
4. Financial Uses	FU_1		FU_2		FU_3		FU_4		FU_5		$FU_{.}$	
5. Financial Sources		FS_1		FS_2		FS_3		FS_4		FS_5		$FS_{.}$
6. Cash and Deposits	D_{11}	C_{11}	D_{12}	C_{12}	D_{13}	C_{13}	D_{14}	C_{14}	D_{15}	C_{15}	$D_{1.}$	$C_{1.}$
7. Other Financial	D_{21}	C_{21}	D_{22}	C_{22}	D_{23}	C_{23}	D_{24}	C_{24}	D_{25}	C_{25}	$D_{2.}$	$C_{2.}$
8. Total Columns	$D_{.1}$	$C_{.1}$	$D_{.2}$	$C_{.2}$	$D_{.3}$	$C_{.3}$	$D_{.4}$	$C_{.4}$	$D_{.5}$	$C_{.5}$	D	C

meaning that it is equal to gross savings minus tangible investment within each sector. From this definition it follows that

$$F_i = FU_i - FS_i \qquad i = 1,5$$

or that financial investment is also equal to financial uses minus financial sources for each sector. This last equality follows from the fact that

$$FU_i = \sum_{j=1}^{2} D_{ji}$$

$$FS_i = \sum_{j=1}^{2} C_{ji}$$

This, and the equality $D_{\cdot i} = C_{\cdot i}$, imply that

$$T_i + FU_i = S_i + FS_i \qquad i = 1,5$$

that is, that

$$F_i = S_i - T_i = FU_i - FS_i$$

Finally, financial investment is also equal to net changes in financial assets minus net changes in financial liabilities. This can be shown as follows. From the debit and credit rules presented in Chapter 2, it follows that FU_i, $i = 1,5$, is equal to the total of all positive increments of financial assets plus the absolute value of all the negative increments of liabilities. With the same basis, FS_i, $i = 1,5$, is equal to the total of the absolute value of all negative increments of financial assets plus all positive increments of liabilities. These relationships could be written as:

$$FU_i = \sum(+\text{financial assets}) + \sum|-\text{liabilities}|$$

$$FS_i = \sum|-\text{financial assets}| + \sum(+\text{liabilities})$$

where the straight parentheses denote absolute value. It follows that $F_i = \Sigma(+ \text{ financial assets}) - \Sigma|-\text{financial assets}| - \Sigma(+\text{liabilities}) - \Sigma|\text{liabilities}|)$. It should be observed that these net changes could be either positive or negative.

The net changes in financial assets for the nonbank sectors can be further broken down into net changes in money and deposits, plus net changes in nonmonetary financial assets. Liabilities, as usual, include only nonmonetary financial claims.

The net changes in nonmonetary financial assets minus those in liabilities represent the resources given in credit if the difference is positive, and received as credit if the difference is negative.

12.2 The Interpretation of the Flow of Funds Statement

The FFS is usually presented as a detailed accounting description of savings and investment in an economy. It is further assumed that the investments appearing in the FFS will contribute to increases in the production capacity of an economy.

A first difficulty with this characterization is that, as observed previously, the FFS statement is a summary of the financial aspects in all the transactions that take place in an economy. This means that it includes the financial components of transactions involving exchanges of goods and services regardless of whether they are used for consumption, current production, or investment. The FFS also records exchanges of financial resources through loans and their payments, regardless of whether the resources so exchanged are used for investment.

A second difficulty originates in the fact that in economics it is frequently assumed that all investment is a consequence of an actual action on the part of an investor, and has as its objective an increase in the productive capacity of the economy. However, the definition of investment in the FFS differs from the one just presented. Tangible investment in the FFS is simply the difference between production and consumption. As already observed, it will always be equal to gross savings. However, this tangible investment includes, on the one hand, the desired investment oriented towards increased production (to be called active investment) and on the other hand, the not-desired, or passive, investment, that is, the increase in inventories due to lack of sales that are likely to deter future production.

The purpose of the interpretation of the qualities appearing in the FFS statement is to evaluate whether the tangible investment recorded will contribute to increased production capacity and to specify the source of that active investment.

In the presentation here, the transactions will be classified in the following groups:

1. those between economic units in the private sector of a closed economy and affecting both real and financial aspects;
2. those between economic units in the private sector of a closed economy and affecting only financial aspects;
3. those between the private sector and the government; and
4. those between homeland economy and rest of the world.

The financial assets and liabilities will be subdivided in the following four groups:

1. cash and deposits (D_{1i}, C_{1i})
2. consumer credit (D_{2i}, C_{2i})
3. short-term (D_{3i}, C_{3i})
4. long-term (D_{4i}, C_{4i})

It will also be assumed that consumer credit transfers goods and services from industry to households only for consumption purposes; that short-term credit transfers financial resources from households or the financial sector to industry for production or current expenditures; and that long-term credit is used only for active investment.

Transactions between Private Economic Units Affecting Both Real and Financial Aspects of a Closed Economy

1. All the transactions involving money, with the exception of those exchanges involving cash for deposits, or vice versa, are included in this group.

If an economy had only this type of transaction, that is, if the debits and credits of other financial assets and liabilities were zero, we would have

$$F_i = FU_i - FS_i = D_{1i} - C_{1i}$$

That is, all the financial investment would be equal to the positive or negative balance of money.

When only households, industry, and banks are considered, it follows from the fact that $\Sigma F_i = 0$, and that $D_{i1} \geq C_{i1}$ for $i = 1,2$, that industry has to deplete its deposits. The possibility of the banking system increasing its money liabilities and passing them to industry is excluded by the assumption that all nonmonetary assets and liabilities are zero.

2. Transactions involving consumer credit, that is, purchases and sales on credit of consumer goods and services, are in this group.

In Table 12–3, which outlines the effect of this type of transaction, it can be seen that a sale on credit of $\$k_2$ increases the consumer credit liabilities of households and assets of industry. It also reduces the gross savings of households and, with the assumption that all the sale is nondistributed profit, increases the gross savings of industry. The gross savings of the economy in this special case would not be affected.

Table 12–3 also shows the effect of consumer credit provided to households in money by the banking system.

Table 12–3
Effect on the FFS of Transactions Involving Consumer Credit[a]

	Households		Industry		Banks		Total Rows	
	Debit	Credit	Debit	Credit	Debit	Credit	Debit	Credit
Gross Savings		$S_1+k_2-k_3$		$S_2+k_2+k_3$		S_3		
Tangible Investment	T_1		T_1		T_3			
Cash and Deposits	$D_{11}+k_3$	$C_{11}+k_3$	$D_{12}+k_3$	C_{12}	D_{13}	$C_{13}+k_3$	$D_{1.}+2k_3$	$C_{1.}+2k_3$
Consumer Credit	D_{21}	$C_{21}+k_2+k_3$	$D_{22}+k_2$	C_{22}	$D_{23}+k_3$	C_{23}	$D_2+k_2+k_3$	$C_2+k_2+k_3$
Total	$D_{.1}+k_3$	$C_{.1}+k_3$	$D_{.2}+k_2+k_3/C_{.2}+k_2+k_3$		$D_{.3}+k_3$	$C_{.3}+k_3$	$D+k_2+3k_3$	$C+k_2+3k_3$

[a]In this table the rows and columns directly affected by the transaction are presented. The others remain as in Table 12–2.

Transactions between Private Units Affecting Only the
Financial Aspects of a Closed Economy

1. Transactions involving loans from household to industry, directly or through banking and financing, are in this group.

The simplest case in which firms in the production sectors are able to sell the part of the production not consumed by Hh is when Hh pass their savings to the production sector through long-term nonmonetary financial instruments. In this case, Hh money and deposits would be low, and nonmonetary financial investments high. The production sector would have high liabilities and high levels of money and deposits. In the situation described, the supply of money, that is, the monetary liabilities of the banks, can remain constant. That is, their value would be zero in the FFS since its records only increments.

A comparison of the cases in which households do ($k_1 > 0$) and do not ($k_1 = 0$) invest in long-term nonmonetary financial assets appears in Table 12–4. In this table it is clear that the values of T_i, S_i, and F_i for $i = 1,2$ do not change, and, as a result, those of $T.$, $S.$, and $F.$ also remain constant. Despite this, Hh long-term financial assets can increase in k_1, and, at the same time, industries have additional resources for investment.

A variation of the case just described which also appears in Table 12–4 is the following: Hh pass k_2 of their money and deposits through nonmonetary financial assets to the banks and other financial intermediaries, and these economic units are the ones that provide, through loans, the k_2 resources needed by industry.

It should be observed that the effects of short-term financing would appear in the FFS statement in a form identical to that of long-term financing. This means that, if no information is available on whether the assets acquired by households are short- or long-term, it would not be possible to specify whether the resources passed to industry were used for current production or for investment.

2. Transactions involving loans from the banking and financial system to industry, financed with the creation of new money, are in this group.

Another possible way to invest Hh savings in order to increase future production is through the creation of new money and deposits. In this case, the financial investment of Hh can include a substantial amount of money and deposits. However, new money created by the banking system could be passed to the production sector, increasing the nonmonetary financial assets of the banks and the liabilities of production firms. The effects of these transactions on the FFS are presented in Table 12–5.

It might seem surprising that in the case under consideration, in which it appears that, on the one hand, households retain their savings, and on the other, firms use theirs, real savings remain equal to real investment.

Table 12–4
Effect on the FFS of Transactions Involving Long-term Financing from Households to Industry Directly or Through Banking and Financing[a]

	Households		Industry		Banking		Total	
	Debit	Credit	Debit	Credit	Debit	Credit	Debit	Credit
Gross Savings	T_1	S_1	T_2	S_2	T_3	S_3	$T.$	$S.$
Tangible Investment								
Cash and Deposits	D_{11}	$C_{11}+k_1+k_2$	$D_{12}+k_1+k_2$	C_{12}	$D_{13}+k_2$	$C_{13}+k_2$	$D_{1.}+k_1+2k_2$	$C_{1.}+k_1+2k_2$
Long Term Financing	$D_{41}+k_1+k_2$	C_{41}	D_{42}	$C_{42}+k_1+k_2$	$D_{43}+k_2$	$C_{43}+k_2$	$D_{4.}+k_1+2k_2$	$C_{4.}+k_1+2k_2$
Total	$D_{.1}+k_1+k_2$	$C_{.1}+k_1+k_2$	$D_{.2}+k_1+k_2$	$C_{.2}+k_1+k_2$	$D_{.3}+2k_2$	$C_{.3}+2k_2$	$D+2k_1+4k_2$	$C+2k_1+4k_2$

[a]See note for Table 12–3.

Table 12–5
Effect on the FFS of Transactions Involving Long-term Financing through the Creation of New Money[a]

	Households		Industry		Banking		Total Rows	
	Debit	Credit	Debit	Credit	Debit	Credit	Debit	Credit
Gross Savings		S_1		S_2		S_3		$S.$
Tangible Investment	T_1		T_2		T_3		$T.$	
Cash and Deposits	D_{11}	C_{11}	$D_{12}+k$	C_{12}	D_{13}	$C_{13}+k$	$D_{1.}+k$	$C_{1.}+k$
Long Term Financing	D_{41}	C_{41}	D_{42}	C_{42}	$D_{43}+k$	C_{43}	$D_{4.}+k$	$C_{4.}+k$
Total Columns	$D_{.1}$	$C_{.1}$	$D_{.2}+k$	$C_{.2}+k$	$D_{.3}+k$	$C_{.3}+k$	$D+2k$	$C+2k$

[a]See note for Table 12–3.

The basic reason for this is clearly that households retain only the money and deposits value of their savings, not their real counterparts. If they decided to use these monetary resources, prices would increase; that is, the excess of money and deposits would be eliminated through inflation.

3. Transactions involving direct credit from producers to investors are in this group. Another possibility for transferring real resources is through direct credit from producers to investors. However, if producers are not able to use the nonmonetary financial assets created in this way to obtain the cash and deposits needed in their production process, this alternative is not likely to be used, and no further analysis of it will be made here.

A similar analysis can be made assuming that the government absorbs savings from households and uses them for investment goods produced by industry. The government can also obtain resources from the banking system and compete with the private sector for the goods and services available, thereby increasing their prices.

Transactions Involving the Rest of the World

Finally, the influence on the allocation of savings to investment of transactions with rest of the world will be considered. A special characteristic of RW is that usually all its gross savings must be transformed into financial investment, that is, the possibility of tangible investment for RW can be considered nonexistent. In principle, any positive gross savings by RW can be balanced with loans made by RW to homeland. This means that RW can increase its financial assets through the use of any of the financial instruments circulating in homeland. This is valid, however, only in the short term. In the long term, positive gross savings of RW are balanced with reductions of gold considered as a financial asset of the banking system. The payments of homeland importers to the central bank balance the reduction of the gold assets which originated in the payments of the central bank to RW.

The important point is that, through the process just described, the savings of households are transformed into increased gold assets of RW, while the tangible assets of homeland industry consist of nondesired inventories that would deter future production. This condition can be avoided if the banking system increases with newly created money the financial resources of industry.

Comparisons of FFS Statements for Different Dates. The preceding observations show that, in order to interpret the FFS statement, one must study the changes in the values appearing in it. In practice, this implies a comparison of statements for different dates. A problem of these comparisons is that such statements would show differences due to changes in the magnitude of the economy as a whole, as well as changes in prices. If it is assumed that changes in prices affect all nonmonetary financial assets and liabilities equally, it is possible to study the differences between several FFS statements by comparing the relative values of the quantities appearing in them. In the notation being used, this implies a comparison for different dates of the values of the proportions

$$D_{hi}/D_{\cdot i}$$

$$C_{hi}/C_{\cdot i}$$

for the columns, and for the rows:

$$D_{hi}/D_{h\cdot}$$

$$C_{hi}/C_{h\cdot}$$

From these definitions of the proportions it follows that, if all the components D_{hi} and C_{hi} change at a common rate, the values of the proportions do not change. On the other hand, the observation of the change in the values of the proportions from one date to the next can be used to determine whether tangible investment is active and whether this investment is financed by the savings of households or by new money created by the banking system.

12.3 Forecasting the Flow of Funds Statement When Tangible Investment Changes Exogenously

The observations made so far with respect to the FFS show how it is possible to follow only some of the quantities that appear in it. They do not permit any estimation of how the whole table would be modified when one of its components changes. A method that can be used for this estimation will be presented here.

The first step is to put the FFS in computational form, as is done in Tables 12–6 and 12–7. The data for Table 12–1 are used in Table 12–6, and Table 12–7 presents the notation to be used, taking Table 12–2 as a point of departure.

In the presentation here it will be assumed that there are J sectors in the economy and P financial assets with corresponding liabilities. In the example for this chapter, $J = 5$ and $P = 7$.

Row j of the matrices $[D_{jp}]$ (transpose of the matrix $[D_{pj}]$), $[T]$, and $[DR]$ is the debit column of sector j in the FFS. This means that $[D_{jp}]$ is a $J \times P$ matrix whose component D_{jp} is the value of the p financial assets held by economic sector j. For instance, if $j = 2$ and $p = 4$, $D_{jp} = 10$ in Table 12–6, meaning that securities worth \$10 have been acquired by industry. $[T]$ is a column vector with J components. The component T_j is equal to the tangible assets of sector j. $[T]'$ appears as a row in Table 12–2. $[DR]$ is a column vector with J components, equal to the totals of debits for sector J. $[DR]'$ appears as the last row in Table 12–2.

By definition

$$[D_{jp}][1] + [T] = [DR] \tag{12.1}$$

since $[DR]$ has as components the totals of the debit columns of the economic sectors in the FFS.

Similarly, column j of the matrices $[C_{pj}]$, $[S]'$, and $[CR]'$ is the credit column of sector j in the FFS. This means that $[C_{pj}]$ is a $P{\times}J$ matrix whose component C_{pj} is the value of claim p against sector j. $[S]'$ is a row vector that has as components S_j the value of sectors gross savings. It appears as a row in both Tables 12–2 and 12–6.

Finally, as before,

$$[C_{pj}]'[1] + [S] = [CR] \tag{12.2}$$

It should be clear that

$$[D.] = [C.] \tag{12.3}$$

that is, for each row of the FFS, the row total of the debits is equal to the row total of the credits. Also,

$$[DR] = [CR] \tag{12.4}$$

that is, the column total of the debits is equal to the column total of the credits for each sector. (Observe that the components of $[DR]$ and $[CR]$ are denoted with $D.j$ and $C.j$ in Table 12–2.)

In the analysis to be made here, the following proportion is assumed to remain constant between the components of $[D_{jp}]$ and $[D_j.]$ and those of $[C_{pj}]$ and $[CR]$

$$[D]^* = D^*_{jp} = D_{jp}/D_j. \tag{12.5}$$

and

$$[C]^* = C^*_{pj} = C_{pj}/C._p \tag{12.6}$$

To clarify the concepts, the matrices $[D]^*$ and $[C]^*$ for the example for Chapter 12 are presented in Table 12–8.

From equations (12.1) and (12.5) it follows that

$$[DR] = [D]^*[D.]' + [T] \tag{12.7}$$

Table 12–6

Example for Chapter 12: Presentation of FFS in Computable Form

Credits \ Debits	Hh	Ind	Bk	Gov	RW	Cash	Deposits
Households						124.3	581.7
Industry						87.0	580.9
Banks						46.8	81.6
Government						48.7	141.1
Rest of the World						0.0	37.1
Cash	137.2	108.0	36.9	24.7	0.0		
Deposits	551.8	552.0	80.8	180.2	57.6		
Accounts Payable	36.2	11.1	0.0	6.0	3.5		
Securities	10.0	40.0	5.0	0.0	2.0		
Shares	0.0	23.0	3.0	0.0	0.0		
Gov Bonds	5.0	0.0	5.0	15.0	0.0		
Gold	0.0	0.0	10.0	0.0	0.0		
Net Worth	73.6	81.9	4.8	−36.1	0.4		
Totals	813.8	816.0	145.5	189.8	63.5	306.8	1,422.4

and from the definition of $[C_{jp}]$, $[C.]$, and equation (12.6) that

$$[C.] = [C]^* [CR] \tag{12.8}$$

Using equations (12.3), (12.4), (12.7), and (12.8), we obtain

$$[DR] = [D]^* [C]^* [DR] + [T] \tag{12.9}$$

that is,

$$[DR] = [1 - D^*C^*]^{-1} [T] \tag{12.10}$$

where 1 denotes an identity matrix of dimensions $J * J$ and $D^*C^* = [D]^* [C]^*$.

It follows from equations (12.8) and (12.10) that

$$[C.] = [C]^* [1 - D^*C^*]^{-1} [T] \tag{12.11}$$

Also, from equations (12.4) and (12.8) it follows that

$$[C.] = [C]^* [D]^* [D.] + [C^*][T] \tag{12.12}$$

Again using equations (12.3) and (12.12), it follows that

$$[C.] = [1 - C^*D^*]^{-1} [C]^* [T] \tag{12.13}$$

Accounts Receivable	Securities	Shares	Gov Bonds	Gold	Tangible Investments	Total
0.0	47.0	18.0	20.0	0.0	22.8	813.8
42.3	10.0	0.0	0.0	0.0	95.8	816.0
6.1	0.0	0.0	5.0	0.0	6.0	145.5
0.0	0.0	0.0	0.0	0.0	0.0	189.8
8.4	0.0	8.0	0.0	10.0	0.0	63.5
						306.8
						1,422.4
						56.8
						57.0
						26.0
						25.0
						10.0
						124.6
56.8	57.0	26.0	25.0	10.0	124.6	

The inverse matrices in equations (12.10), (12.11), and (12.13) are presented in Table 12–9.

It is possible to evaluate [DR] from equation (12.10), and also to compute [C.] from equation (12.11) or (12.13) when [T] is known.

Once the value of [CR] = [DR] is known, and using equation (12.6), one obtains

$$[C_{jp}] = [C]^*[C\hat{R}] \tag{12.14}$$

where [C$\hat{R}$] is a diagonal matrix with the components of [CR] in the main diagonal, and from the results for [C.] using equation (12.3), the following relationship is determined:

$$[D_{jp}] = [D]'^*[\hat{D}.] \tag{12.15}$$

where [$\hat{D}$.] is a diagonal matrix with the components of [D] in the main diagonal. This means that the procedure just described can be used to estimate the FFS when the values of the tangible assets of all the sectors are exogenously determined. In Table 12–10 a forecast of Table 12–1 is presented.

Table 12–7
Flow of Funds Statement in Computable Form

	Sectors	Transpose Debit Matrix	Tangible Investment	Totals
Sectors		$[D_{pj}]'$	$[T]$	$[DR]$
Credit Matrix	$[C_{pj}]$			$[C.]$
Gross Savings	$[S]'$			$S.$
Totals	$[CR]'$	$[D.]'$	$T.$	

Table 12–8
Example for Chapter 12: Matrices $[D]^*$ and $[C]^*$ for Equations (12.5) and (12.6)

$[D]^*$

0.405	0.409	0.0	0.825	0.692	0.800	0.0
0.284	0.408	0.745	0.175	0.0	0.0	0.0
0.153	0.057	0.107	0.0	0.0	0.200	0.0
0.159	0.099	0.0	0.0	0.0	0.0	0.0
0.0	0.026	0.148	0.0	0.308	0.0	1.0

$[C]^*$

0.169	0.132	0.254	0.130	0.0
0.678	0.676	0.555	0.949	0.907
0.044	0.014	0.0	0.032	0.055
0.012	0.049	0.034	0.0	0.031
0.0	0.028	0.021	0.0	0.0
0.006	0.0	0.034	0.079	0.0
0.0	0.0	0.069	0.0	0.0

Table 12–9
Example for Chapter 12: Inverse Matrices in Equations (12.10), (12.11), and (12.13)

$[1 - D^*C^*]^{-1}$ in Equations (12.10) and (12.11)

7.362	6.316	6.812	8.342	6.922
5.837	6.743	6.162	7.602	6.373
1.134	1.110	2.213	1.482	1.213
1.537	1.513	1.637	2.999	1.658
0.507	0.504	0.605	0.660	1.555

$[1 - C^*D^*]^{-1}$ in Equation (12.13)

3.583	2.508	2.438	2.446	2.466	2.505	2.485
11.907	12.626	11.416	11.255	11.633	11.404	12.429
0.483	0.473	1.455	0.468	0.489	0.472	0.523
0.455	0.448	0.457	1.426	0.438	0.430	0.476
0.205	0.201	0.208	0.188	1.189	0.190	0.200
0.225	0.212	0.199	0.199	0.203	1.209	0.209
0.091	0.083	0.084	0.076	0.078	0.091	1.082

Table 12–10
Projected Flow of Funds Statement

	Households		Industry		Banking		Government		Rest of the World		Total	
	Debit	Credit	Debit	Credit	Debit	Credit	Debit	Credit	Debit	Credit	Debit	Credit
Savings and Deposits		82.8		92.3		5.3		-41.1		0.5		139.8
Tangible Assets	24.2		108.2		4.3		2.1		1.0		139.8	
Cash	139.8	154.3	97.8	121.7	52.6	40.9	54.8	28.1	0.0	0.0	345.1	345.1
Deposits	655.5	620.6	654.6	622.1	92.0	89.6	159.0	205.0	41.8	65.6	1,603.0	1,603.0
Accounts Payable and Receivable	0.0	40.7	47.7	12.5	6.9	0.0	0.0	6.8	9.5	4.0	64.0	64.0
Securities	52.9	11.2	11.3	45.1	0.0	5.5	0.0	0.0	0.0	2.5	64.2	64.2
Shares	20.2	0.0	0.0	25.9	0.0	3.3	0.0	0.0	9.0	0.0	29.2	29.2
Gov Bonds	22.6	5.6	0.0	0.0	5.6	5.5	0.0	17.1	0.0	0.0	28.2	28.2
Financial Gold	0.0	0.0	0.0	0.0	0.0	11.1	0.0	0.0	11.1	0.0	11.1	11.1
Total	915.3	915.3	919.6	919.6	161.4	161.4	215.9	215.9	72.4	72.4	2,284.6	2,284.6

References

Board of Governors of the Federal Reserve System, *Flow of Funds Accounts 1945–1967*, February 1968.

Copeland, M. A., *A Study of Money Flows in the United States*, (New York: National Review of Economic Research, 1952).

Goldsmith, R. W., *The Determinants of Financial Structure* (Paris: OECD, 1966).

Kendrick, J. W., *Economic Accounts and Their Uses* (Chapter 9) (New York: McGraw-Hill, 1972).

Mathews, R., *Accounting for Economists* (Chapter 19) (London: Angus and Robertson, 1969).

Powelson, J. P., *Economic Accounting* (Chapter 25) (New York: McGraw-Hill, 1955).

Stone, R., and Roe, A., *The Financial Interdependence of the Economy, 1957–66* (Chapters II and III) A Program for Growth #11. (Cambridge, England: University of Cambridge, Department of Applied Economics, 1971).

13

Macro-Accounting Statements Dealing with Real Aspects Only: Input-Output Statement (IOS)

13.1 Input-Output Statement (IOS)

The IOS tables are basically a matrix presentation of the income and product statements (IPS) obtained from the lower part of the NTT.

For the preparation of the IOS, the IPS derived from the NTT should present in detail the symmetric debit-credit matrices dealing with intermediate and final goods and services, and with wages, profits, rents, interests, and taxes. On the other hand, only the totals of the debits and credits for each sector are used for sales of capital goods and for changes in inventories. As is usual with the IPS, a row of changes in net worth is included for each sector. For the preparation of the IOS, the quantities of this row always appear in the debit column, with a plus or a minus sign, as required.

The IPS of all the sectors of an economy are then classified in two groups: (a) production sectors, and (b) final demand sectors, including households, government, and rest of the world.

The simplest and, for this reason, the most acceptable way to construct an IOS is to use as columns the debit columns or as rows the credit columns of the IPS for all the sectors of the economy. As observed, for the symmetric debit-credit matrices appearing in the IPS, debits in columns and credits in rows are identical. The part of the IOS corresponding to the symmetric debit-credit matrices included in the IPS and dealing with the production sectors is said to deal with inter-industry transactions and appears on the upper left-hand quadrant of the table. Other organizational details can be seen in the IOS derived from Table 10–1 and presented in Table 13–1. The IOS derived from Table 10–3 for the United States appears in Table 13–2.

In Table 13–1 it is observed that some of the quantities appearing in the IPS are excluded from an IOS. Such deletions, although they are frequently made, do not seem to be justified, and they destroy the systematic approach to the construction of an IOS that has been described.

An alternate procedure that can be used for the construction of an IOS is to use the real transactions statement (RTS) defined in Section 10.6 instead of the IPS. As already observed, in the RTS, additions to net worth are subdivided into tangible assets and financial investment. As presented in Table 13–1, the IOS derived from the RTS also includes this subdivision.

171

Table 13–1
Example for Chapter 13: Input-Output Table (IOT) Derived from NTT in Table 10–1

	Industry	Banking	Increment of Inventory	Investment	Households	Government	Rest of the World (Exports)	Total
Industry	764.8	6.0	15.0	104.6	481.2	74.5	38.5	1484.6
Banking	34.6	6.1	0.0	—	10.1	1.2	0.4	52.6
Rest of the World (Imports)	23.7[a]	0.4	—	6.0	5.9	7.5	—	43.5
Depreciation and Reduction of Inventories	53.7	2.1	—	—	8.7	—	—	64.5
Wages, Profits, Rents, Interest, Taxes	579.4[a]	34.3	—	—	75.2	127.7	4.2	820.8
Additions to Net Worth	23.2	3.7	—	—	64.9[b]	−36.1[b]	0.4[b]	61.1
Net Tangible Investment	42.1[c]	4.9[c]	—	—	14.1[c]	—	—	125.6
Financial Investment	−13.9[c]	−1.2[c]	—	—	+50.8[c]	−36.1[c]	0.4[c]	0.0
Total	1484.6	52.6	15.0	110.6	646.0	174.8	43.5	

[a]23.7 and 579.4 respectively include and exclude wages paid to RW
[b]Usually excluded from current IOT
[c]To be added in IOT obtained from RTS

Table 13–2
United States Input-Output Matrix Derived from Net Worth Part of Table 10–3

	Industry	Finance	Increment of Inventory	Investment	Gov Consumption	Household Consumption	Exports	Total
Industry	764.8	6.0	15.0	104.6	74.5	441.1	38.5	1,444.5
Finance	12.6	6.1			0.2	19.9	0.4	39.2
Imports and Transfers	27.0	0.4			7.5	5.9		40.8
Depreciation	53.7	1.1				8.7		63.5
Reduction Inventories								
Hh Interest	29.3				9.9	12.4		51.6
Hh Dividends	20.1	1.4						21.5
Nondistributed Profits	21.6	3.7						25.3
Rents	19.4							19.4
Wages and Social Insurance	342.4	14.6			76.6	17.9	2.1	453.6
Proprietors Income	59.3							59.3
Transfers to Units	2.7				41.2			43.9
Taxes	91.6	5.9				75.2	2.1	174.8
Totals	1,444.5	39.2	15.0	104.6	209.9	581.1	43.1	2,437.4

It should be clear that IOS having more detail than those just presented here are possible. As examples, the following refinements can be described:

1. A more detailed breakdown of industries and finance can be used.

2. Imports can be disaggregated in imports of industry and of finance, that is, disaggregated according to the breakdown of industries. In this case, each row of the matrix has three components: total, national, and imported.

3. Increases and decreases of inventories can be disaggregated to specify the sector that changes the inventory and the sector that produced the goods held in the inventory. In this case the column and row of inventories become matrices. The matrix for increases in inventories has columns for production and the final sectors. The matrix for decreases in inventories has rows for all the production sectors.

4. The column for investments can be disaggregated into columns for production and final sectors. In this case, each column will specify the goods invested by industrial sector and by sector investing them.

In addition it can be observed that, besides the standard organization of the IOS (that is, the organization in Table 13–1), new organizations could be developed using different forms of aggregation or disaggregation of the symmetric debit-credit matrices in the IPS or the RTS. Thus it follows that, with the proper aggregation, the IOS derived from the RTS can be presented as just the N matrices of the GEE.

Another interesting point is that the financial part of the NTT can, in principle, be "processed" in a form similar to that used for the IOS. This observation is important because, at least at a conceptual level, it makes it possible to extend the methods of analysis developed for the IOS to the financial sectors.

13.2 Some Applications of the IOS

Table 13–3 will be used to show the method of applying the IOS. This table differs from Table 13–1 in the following respects:

1. In Table 13–1 only two production sectors are considered: industry and finance. In Table 13–3, three sectors are considered: primary, manufacture, and services (including finances).

2. Imports are disaggregated in Table 13–3. The possibility of doing this was mentioned in Section 13.1

3. On the other hand, payments to the factors of production, that is, wages, interest, etc., are completely aggregated with depreciation and changes in inventories in Table 13–3.

Table 13–3

Ecuador: Input-Output and National Accounts Statement for 1955 (in 10^6 sucres)

(1) Inputs		Interindustry Transactions				Final Demand				(10) Total
		Primary Sector (2)	Manufacture (3)	Services (4)	Total Inputs (5)	Investment (6)	Households and Governments (7)	Rest of the World (8)	Total (9)	
Primary Sector	Total	211	854	—	1,065	73	3,139	1,792	5,004	6,069
	National	207	612	—	819	71	3,103	1,792	4,966	5,785
	Imported	4	242	—	246	2	36	—	38	284
Manufacture	Total	296	1,061	218	1,575	736	3,181	65	3,982	5,557
	National	265	843	218	1,326	144	2,804	65	3,013	4,339
	Imported	31	218	—	249	592	377	—	969	1,218
Services	Total	1,518	478	—	1,996	997	2,847	214	4,058	6,054
	National	1,498	316	—	1,814	780	2,696	214	3,690	5,504
	Imported	20	162	—	182	217	151	—	368	550
Payments to the Factors of Production		3,760	1,946	5,286			9,167			10,992
Total		5,785	4,339	5,504		2,071		1,806		28,672

In summary, two matrices are presented in Table 13–3: first, the matrix of use of national production for raw materials of final uses (rows 2, 5, and 8 of Table 13–3 and see Table 13–4), and second, the matrix of imported raw materials and imported goods for final use (rows 3, 6, and 9 in Table 13–3).

13.2.1 Use of the Input-Output Matrix of National Production

The notation to be used for the matrix of national production is the following (the time subindex is omitted):

P_j = total national production (inputs plus final uses) of sector j. Vector in column (10) in the right-hand side of Table 13–4.

DN_{jh} = national production sold by sector j to sector h. The DN_{jh} constitute the matrix of interindustrial uses of national production. They appear in columns (2) to (4) at the left-hand side of Table 13–4.

CN_j = consumption of national goods by sector j. Vector in column (7) of Table 13–4.

IN_j = gross investment of national production by sector j. Vector in column (6) of Table 13–4.

X_j = exports from sector j. Vector in column (8) of Table 13–4.

E_j = total final uses of production by sector j. Vector in column (9) of Table 13–4.

DN_j = total production of sector j used as raw materials. Vector in column (5) of Table 13–4.

The following relationships can be established for the variables in Table 13–4, and in general for any IOS:

$$P_j = E_j + DN_j \qquad (13.1)$$

or, in matrix notation

$$[P] = [E] + [DN]$$

It is also possible to write

$$DN_j = \sum_{h=1}^{n} DN_{jh} \qquad (13.2)$$

Table 13–4
Ecuador: Input-Output Matrix of National Production

j	DN_{ji}	DN_{j2}	DN_{j3}	DN_j	IN_j	CN_j	X_j	E_j	P_j
(1)	(2)	(3)	(4)	(5)	(6)	(7)	(8)	(9)	(10)
1	207	612	—	819	71	3,103	1,792	4,966	5,785
2	265	843	218	1,362	144	2,804	65	3,013	4,339
3	1,498	316	—	1,814	780	2,696	214	3,690	5,504

A basic element in input-output analysis is the relationship

$$A_{jh} = DN_{jh}/P_h \tag{13.3}$$

with the assumption that the A_{jh} are constant in time. (See, however, Section 13.2.3). An A_{jh} is the input demanded by sector h from sector j to produce one unit of output (of sector h).

In the case of the input-output matrix of national production in Table 13–4, the matrix $[A]$ takes the following form:

$$[A] = \begin{bmatrix} 0.035782 & 0.141046 & 0.000000 \\ 0.045808 & 0.194284 & 0.039608 \\ 0.258946 & 0.072828 & 0.000000 \end{bmatrix}$$

Using the definition for the A_{jh}, equation (13.2) can be written

$$DN_j = \sum_{h=1}^{n} A_{jh} \times P_h$$

or, using matrix notation,

$$[DN]_t = [A] \times [P]_t. \tag{13.4}$$

Equation (13.4) is frequently used in disaggregated analyses. Perhaps the most common application is to estimate $[P]$ when $[A]$ and $[E]$ are known.

From equations (13.1) to (13.3), in usual algebraic notation, one obtains

$$E_j = P_j - \sum_{h=1}^{n} A_{jh} \times P_h$$

and, passing to the notation of matrices and vectors,

$$[E] = [1 - A] \times [P] \tag{13.5}$$

where $[1 - A]$ denotes the matrix obtained by subtracting the matrix $[A]$ from the identity matrix. Equation (13.5) is an abbreviated expression of a system of n equations with the n values of P_j as unknowns. The meaning of this system is that, given the values of the $[E]$ and $[A]$ matrices, those of $[P]$ can be computed. (It can be shown that the matrix $[1 - A]$ has an inverse for all $[A]$ that make economic sense.)

From the matrix $[A]$ previously presented, one obtains

$$[1 - A] = \begin{bmatrix} 0.964218 & -0.141046 & 0.000000 \\ -0.045808 & 0.805716 & -0.039608 \\ -0.258946 & -0.072828 & 1.000000 \end{bmatrix}$$

Given the values of $[E]$, equation (13.5) can be solved in several ways. One of these is the inversion of the matrix $[1 - A]$. The inverse of matrix $[1 - A]$ is

$$[1 - A]^{-1} \begin{bmatrix} 1.047814 & 0.184086 & 0.007291 \\ 0.073172 & 1.258447 & 0.049844 \\ 0.276656 & 0.139318 & 1.005518 \end{bmatrix}$$

Utilizing this matrix, equation (13.5) can be written

$$[P] = [1 - A]^{-1} \times [E] \tag{13.6}$$

In summary, the use of an input-output matrix makes it possible to determine the national production in each sector of the economy needed to satisfy a known final demand for the production of each sector. In order to project total production by sector, projection of the final uses of the production of each sector are needed. Methods for such a projection are based on the use of sectoral consumption functions. Estimated values of $[P]$ for a given $[E]$ are presented in Table 13–5.

Another interesting property of input-output matrices will be explained here. For this, let SE = total production in final uses, that is,

$$SE = \sum_{j=1}^{n} E_j$$

Using matrix notation it is possible to write

$$[E] = SE \times [E_1/SE, E_2/SE, \ldots, E_n/SE]$$

Table 13–5
Estimation of [P] For Exogenous [E] with Equation (13.6)

[E]	[P]
5,320	6,758
6,240	8,482
4,820	7,188

where the vector $[E_1/SE, E_2/SE, \ldots, E_n/SE]$, to be denoted by E/SE, is the normalized form of the vector E, that is, each of the components of this vector is divided by SE so that the sum of the normalized vector is one.

The use of the normalized vector makes it possible to break down the estimation of total production required to satisfy a final demand of SE into two parts. First the vector

$$[1 - A]^{-1} \times [E/SE]$$

is computed. This gives the total production by sector needed to satisfy a final demand for consumption goods equal to one. Second, the total production by sector needed to satisfy the total demand SE is obtained by multiplying the vector by SE.

13.2.2 Use of the Input-Output Matrix of Imported Goods

As in the case of the input-output matrix for national production, the basic step here is to relate imports of intermediate goods to total production. For this, let DM_j denote imports of raw materials by sector j, and Z_{jh} denote goods produced by RW sector j and used as raw materials by homeland sector h. Thus

$$DM_j = \sum_{h=1}^{n} Z_{jh} \tag{13.7}$$

The elements of the matrix $[V]$ of technical coefficients of imports are defined by

$$V_{jh} = Z_{jh}/P_h$$

that is, V_{jh} is the volume of production from sector j that is imported by sector h in order to produce one unit of its product.

From the matrix in Table 13–3 one obtains

$$[V] = \begin{bmatrix} 0.000691 & 0.055773 & 0.000000 \\ 0.005359 & 0.050242 & 0.000000 \\ 0.003457 & 0.037336 & 0.000000 \end{bmatrix}$$

Using the definition of $[V]$, equation (13.7) can be written

$$[DM] = [V] \times [P] \tag{13.8}$$

This equation makes it possible to estimate $[DM]$ when $[P]$ is known.

13.2.3 Changes in the Components of Input-Output Matrices

In Section 13.2.1 two types of input-output matrices were introduced. They appear as in equation (13.4):

$$[DN]_t = [A] \times [P]_t$$

and

$$[DM]_t = [V] \times [P]_t \tag{13.9}$$

The notation used in these two equations indicates that their matrices do not change in time. However, this assumption does not hold for long-term analysis.

There are numerous methods for changing the components of matrices $[A]$ and $[V]$. From the computational point of view, the method to be called here "QAS" is particularly interesting. This method will be explained with respect to matrix $[A]$. It remains the same with respect to matrix $[V]$, except for obvious changes in notation.

According to the QAS method, matrix $[A]_1$ is obtained from matrix $[A]_0$ with the equation

$$[A]_1 = [Q1] \times [A]_0 \times [S1] \tag{13.10}$$

where $[Q1]$ is a diagonal matrix whose q_{1ii} element, to be denoted by q_{1i}, reflects the influences that affect all uses of product i as input, and $[S1]$ is a diagonal matrix whose element s_{1jj}, to be denoted by s_{1j}, reflects the influences that affect all the inputs of industry j.

The reason for the description of q_{1i} and s_{1j} is that the ith row of $[A]_1$ is the vector

$$[q_{1i}s_{i1}A_{0i1}, q_{1i}s_{i2}A_{0i2}, \ldots, q_{1i}s_{in}A_{0in}]$$

that is, the component q_{1i} of matrix $[Q1]$ affects all the components of the ith row of matrix $[A]_0$. At this point it should be observed that the components of row i and column j of matrix $[A]_0$ are the quantity of product i needed to produce one unit of output of product j.

Column j of the matrix $[A]_1$ has the form

$$q_{11}s_{1j}A_{01j}$$

$$q_{12}s_{1j}A_{02j}$$

$$\vdots$$

$$q_{1n}s_{1j}A_{0nj}$$

More specifically, q_{1i} could reflect, for instance, changes in the supply of product i, while s_{1j} reflected changes in management practices in industry j.

Using matrix algebra it can be observed that the following equation holds:

$$[A]_t = [Q1]^t \times [A]_0 \times [S1]^t = [q^t_{1i}s^t_{1j}A_{0ij}] \tag{13.11}$$

The equation shows that q_{1i} and s_{1j} are indices of the trends that affect the components of a matrix of technical coefficients. In addition, the values of the q_{1i} and s_{1j} can be estimated with simple statistical techniques.

In the case of the matrix $[V]$, we have

$$[V]_t = [Q2]^t \times [V]_0 \times [S2]^t = [q^t_{2i}s^t_{2j}V^t_{0i1}] \tag{13.12}$$

14

Macro-Accounting Statements Dealing with Real Aspects Only: The Income and Product (IPS) and the Saving and Investment (SVS) Statements

14.1 Content of this Chapter

This chapter deals with two types of consolidated statements for the economy as a whole:

1. The income and product statements, whose object is to show the value of all goods and services produced by a macro-economic unit
2. The saving and investment statement, which shows the additions to net worth, that is, national capital and national wealth, for the economy as a whole

Special attention will be given to the income and product statements.

The income and product statements are derived from the net worth part of the NTT only. As a starting point, the income and product statements of each sector are presented systematically in one table. Then assumptions about fictitious transactions are made. With these transactions, production activities are concentrated on a consolidated production sector, while the other sectors receive only the income generated by the production process, or spend that income to purchase goods and services.

This approach will be modified here. Rather than using only the net worth part of the NTT, the whole NTT will be used as a starting point. The effect of the fictitious transactions needed to consolidate production in both the financial and real parts of the NTT will be studied. In this way, an NTT integrated with the income and product statements will be obtained.

The justification for this approach is that the national income and product statement is used as a starting point in most macro-economic models. As a result, in order to integrate the financial aspects of an economy into the macro-economic models, it is necessary to prepare an NTT that includes the income and product statement, as just described.

183

14.2 Integration of the NTT and the Income and Product Statement

The integration of the NTT and the IPS begins with Table 10–2. This table is reproduced, with some reclassification of information, in Table 14–1. The most important modifications of Table 10–2 are as follows:

1. The value of tangible assets is obtained by adding purchases of capital and changes in inventories presented in Table 10–2.
2. The values of HL and RW final consumption, intermediate goods, investment, and changes in inventories are presented separately in Table 14–1. (This step is needed mainly for model construction.)
3. Income from work, that is, wages, is separated from income from capital, that is, profits, rents, and interests, and from taxes in Table 14–1.

As a second step, all the accounts of production units are aggregated in one production sector account. In the case of the example for this chapter, only industry and banking are aggregated. The results obtained are presented in Table 14–2.

The next step is to aggregate in the production sector all the values produced by households, government, and rest of the world. This process will be explained here, using as an example the information in Table 14–2.

1. In Table 14–2 *households are producers* only to the extent that they receive the income and pay the cost of operating capital goods. In Table 14–2 this activity reduces, on the one hand, to the purchase of tangible assets, and on the other, to the reduction of those assets by capital consumption and depreciation. In actual national accounting, it is assumed that the use of their own home is a rent received by households and produced by the tangible assets they use. This important production of the households' tangible assets will not be considered here.

To transfer the production activities of households to the production sector, it will be assumed that households lend all their tangible assets in kind to production. For the period covered by the transactions studied here, households would lend only the $22.8 of tangible assets that appear in Table 14–2. All other tangible assets are covered in previous periods. The loan of tangible assets is recorded in the household accounts with a reduction (credit) to tangible assets and an increase (debit) to financial assets. On the other hand, producers increase (debit) tangible assets and increase (credit) liabilities.

Since the production sector now contains all the tangible assets of the HL sector, the depreciation of these assets will affect the production sector. The $8.7 of depreciation is eliminated from the HL account, credited to capital consumption, and debited to depreciation of production.

Table 14–1
Example for Chapter 14: National Transactions Table (Modification of Table 10–2)

	Households		Industry		Banking		Government		Rest of the World		Total	
	Debit	Credit	Debit	Credit	Debit	Credit	Debit	Credit	Debit	Credit	Debit	Credit
Tangible Assets	22.8		95.8		6.0						124.6	
Capital Consumption		8.7		53.7		1.1						63.5
Cash	124.3	137.2	87.0	108.0	46.8	36.9	48.7	24.7			306.8	306.8
Deposits	581.7	551.8	580.9	552.0	81.6	80.8	141.1	180.2	37.1	57.6	1,422.4	1,422.4
Other Financial Assets and Liabilities	85.0	51.2	52.3	74.1	11.1	23.0		21.0	26.4	5.5	174.8	174.8
HL Final Consumption	491.3			555.7		11.3	75.7				567.0	567.0
RW Final Consumption	5.9						7.5			13.4	13.4	13.4
HL Intermediate Goods			799.6	770.8	6.0	34.8					805.6	805.6
RW Intermediate Goods			20.1	38.5	0.4	0.4			38.9	20.5	59.4	59.4
HL Sales Capital Goods				104.6							104.6	104.6
HL Change in Inventories				15.0	1.0						1.0	15.0
Depreciation	8.7		53.7		1.1						63.5	
RW Sales Capital Goods										6.0		6.0
RW Change Inventories												
Wages		547.4	412.9		14.6		117.8		2.1		547.4	547.4
Profits, Rents, Interests		98.6	78.5		13.8		9.9			3.6	102.2	102.2
Taxes	75.2		91.6		5.9			174.8	2.1		174.8	174.8
Total	1,394.9	1,394.9	2,272.4	2,272.4	188.3	188.3	400.7	400.7	106.6	106.6		

Table 14–2
Example for Chapter 14: National Transactions Table with Industry and Banking Consolidated

	Households		Industry and Banking		Government		Rest of the World		Total	
	Debit	Credit	Debit	Credit	Debit	Credit	Debit	Credit	Debit	Credit
Tangible Assets Capital Consumption	22.8	8.7	101.8	54.8					124.6	63.5
Cash	124.3	137.2	133.8	144.9	48.7	24.7			306.8	306.8
Deposits	581.7	551.8	662.5	632.8	141.1	180.2	37.1	57.6	1,422.4	1,422.4
Other Financial Assets and Liabilities	85.0	51.2	63.4	97.1		21.0	26.4	5.5	174.8	174.8
HL Final Sales and Consumption	491.3			567.0	75.7				567.0	567.0
RW Final Consumption	5.9				7.5			13.4	13.4	13.4
HL Intermediate			805.6	805.6					805.6	805.6
RW Intermediate			20.5	38.9			38.9	20.5	59.4	59.4
HL Capital Goods				104.6						104.6
HL Change Inventories			1.0	15.0					1.0	15.0
RW Capital Goods								6.0		6.0
RW Change Inventories									0.0	0.0
Depreciation	8.7		54.8						63.5	
Wages		547.4	427.5		117.8		2.1		547.4	547.4
Profits, Rents, Interests		98.6	92.3		9.9			3.6	102.2	102.2
Taxes	75.2		97.5			174.8	2.1		174.8	174.8
Total	1,394.9	1,394.9	2,460.7	2,460.7	400.7	400.7	106.6	106.6	4,362.9	4,362.9

As payments for the use of the HL assets, the production sector pays to households a rent, assumed to be equal to the cost that production pays for the use of the assets, that is, the $8.7 for its depreciation.

Finally, households pay for the use of the tangible assets they rented to the production sector. As a result, sales and final consumption increase by $8.7.

2. As observed, all the government activities that result in the production of goods that are sold to the public are included in the production sector. As a result, there are no market prices to evaluate government output. It is assumed that its value is equal to that of wages, salaries, and interests paid by the government. These activities are assumed, for the preparation of the national income and production statement, to be performed by the production sector. This means that the wages, salaries, and interests paid by the government are now paid by the production sector. On the other hand, government purchases the services produced with those expenses from the production sector.

3. It is also assumed that only the production sector directly handles transactions of goods and services with the rest of the world. As a result, all imports or exports of households and government would now be "purchased" from the production sector, which also purchases them from RW.

Imports of households are thus added to consumption expenditures by that sector. A similar transformation is made in the case of government.

It is assumed that taxes and wages paid by the rest of the world sector are paid by the production sector of the economy and then included among exports to RW.

Similar assumptions are made with respect to capital goods purchased from RW. In Table 14–2 they appear as credits for RW, compensated for by some transfer of financial assets. In the national income and product account, it is assumed that capital goods are purchased and sold only by the production sector.

The results obtained with the transformations just described are presented in Table 14–3. The changes are explained in detail in the notes on this table.

14.3 The National Income and Product (NIP) Statement

14.3.1 Accounting Form of the Statement

The lower part of Table 14–3 includes the NIP statement for the four sectors considered in the economy. The statement for the production sector is usually presented as a consolidation of intermediate goods and ser-

Table 14–3

Example for Chapter 14: Integrated National Transactions Table and National and Sectoral Income and Product Statement

	Households		Production	
	Debit	*Credit*	*Debit*	*Credit*
Gross Savings[a]		73.6[a]		23.2[a(1)]
Tangible Assets	0.0[(2)]		124.6[(3)]	
Capital Consumption		0.0[(4)]		63.5[(5)]
Cash	124.3	137.2	133.8	144.9
Deposits	581.7	551.8	662.5	632.8
Other	107.8[(6)]	51.2	63.4	119.9[(7)]
Total Flow of Funds[a]	813.8[a]	813.8[a]	984.3[a]	984.3[a]
HL Final Consumption	500.0[(8)]			703.4[(9)]
RW Final Consumption	5.9		13.4	13.4
HL Intermediate Goods			805.6	805.6
RW Intermediate			20.5	43.1[(11)]
HL Capital Goods				104.6
HL Change Inventories				14.0
RW Capital Goods			6.0[(12)]	6.0[(12)]
RW Change Inventories				
Depreciation	0.0[(13)]		63.5[(14)]	
Wages		547.4	547.4[(15)]	
Profits, Rents, Interests		107.3[(18)]	110.9[(19)]	
Taxes	75.2		99.6[(21)]	
Total	1,394.9	1,394.9	2,651.2	2,651.2
Total Only Net Worth[b]	581.1[b]	654.7[b]	1,666.9[b]	1,690.1[b]
Gross Savings[b]	73.6[b]		23.2[b]	
Total[b]	654.7[b]	654.7[b]	1,690.1[b]	1,690.1[b]

[a] Appear only in FFS and not in NTT.

[b] Appear only in income and product accounts and not in NTT.

Special Notes to Table 14–3 ("In text" preceded by a number refers to the numbered paragraphs in Section 14.2.):

(1) 31.9 Table 21–1
     −8.7 1 in text
     23.2

(2) See 1 in text

(3) 101.8 Table 14–2
     +22.8 1 in text
     124.6

(7) 97.1 Table 14–2
     22.8 1 in text
     119.9

(8) 491.3 Table 14–2
     8.7 1 in text
     500.0

(9) 567.0 Table 14–2
     8.7 1 in text
     117.8 2 in text
     9.9 2 in text
     703.4

(13) See 1 in text

(14) 54.8 Table 14–2
     8.7 1 in text
     63.5

(15) 427.5 Table 14–2
     117.8 2 in text
     2.1 3 in text
     547.4

(19) 92.3 Table 14–2
     8.7 1 in text
     9.9 2 in text
     110.9

(20) See 2 in text

(21) 97.5 Table 14–2
     2.1 3 in text
     99.6

Government		Rest of the World		Total	
Debit	Credit	Debit	Credit	Debit	Credit
	−36.1[a]		.4[a]		61.1[a]
				124.6	
					63.5
48.7	24.7			306.8	306.8
141.1	180.2	37.1	57.6	1,422.4	1,422.4
	21.0	26.4	5.5	197.6	197.6
189.8[a]	189.8[a]	63.5[a]	63.5[a]	2,051.4	2,051.4
203.4[10]				703.4	703.4
7.5			13.4	26.8	26.8
				805.6	805.6
		43.1[11]	20.5	63.6	63.6
					104.6
					14.0
			6.0	6.0	12.0
				63.5	
0.0[16]		0.0[17]		547.4	547.4
0.0[20]			3.6	110.9	110.9
	174.8	0.0[22]		174.8	174.8
400.7	400.7	106.6	106.6	4,553.4	4,553.4
210.9[b]	174.8[b]	43.1[b]	43.5[b]	2,502.0[b]	2,563.1[b]
−36.1[b]		0.4[b]		61.1[b]	
174.8[b]	174.8[b]	43.5[b]	43.5[b]	2,563.1[b]	2,563.1[b]

(4)	See 1 in text	(5)	54.8 Table 14–2
			  8.7 1 in text
			63.5
				(6)	85.0 Table 4–2
					  22.8 1 in text
					107.8

(10)	75.7 Table 14–2
	117.8 1 in text
	  9.9
	203.4
		(11)	38.9 Table 14–2
			  2.1 3 in text
			  2.1 3 in text
			43.1
				(12)	See 3 in text

(16)	See 2 in text	(17)	See 3 in text	(18)	98.6 Table 14–2 8.7 1 in text 107.3
(22)	See 3 in text				

Table 14–4
United States Summary National Income and Product Accounts, 1966
(10⁹ 1966 dollars)

	Personal Income and Outlay Accounts		National Income and Product Accounts		Government Receipts and Expenditures		Foreign Transactions Accounts	
	Debit	*Credit*	*Debit*	*Credit*	*Debit*	*Credit*	*Debit*	*Credit*
Personal Outlays								
Personal consumption expenditures	465.9			465.9				
Interest paid by consumers	12.4	12.4						
Personal transfer payments for foreigners (government)	0.6							0.8
Personal Interest Income (except paid by consumer)		30.0	20.2		9.9			
Dividends (1–14,2–11)[a]		21.5	21.5					
Rental Income of Persons		19.4	19.4					
Wages, Salaries and Other Labor Income (1–3,1–7)[a]		415.4	415.4					
Proprietor Income		59.3	59.3					
Transfer Payments to Persons (2, 16i)[a]		43.9	2.9		41.2			
Personal contributions for social insurance	17.9					17.9		
Government Purchases of Goods and Services			154.3	154.3	154.3			

	601.8	601.9	743.5	743.3	213.1	213.0	43.0	43.2
(Transfer Payments to Foreigners)								2.3
Subsidies Loss Current Surplus of Government Enterprises (k–21, 3–6)[a]			−2.2		2.3	2.2		
Taxes (1–12, 1–20, 2–1, 3–10, 3–11, 3–12)[a]	75.2		99.6			174.8		
Employer Contributions to Social Insurance (1–6)			20.3			20.3		
Fixed Investments				104.6				
Change in Business Inventories				13.4				
Capital Consumption Allowance			63.5					
Net Export of Goods and Services				5.1			43.0	37.9
Inventory Valuation Adjustment			−1.6					
Personal Savings	29.8							
Undistributed Profits			27.8					
Statistical discrepancy			−2.6					
Surplus or Deficit (−) National Income and Product Accounts					3.2			
Net Foreign Investment								2.2
Totals	601.8	601.9	743.5	743.3	213.1	213.0	43.0	43.2

Source: _Survey of Current Business, July 1967_: Personal Income Table 2; National Income Table 1; Government Receipts Table 3; Foreign Transactions Table 4.

[a] Numbers in parentheses refer to table and line numbers from which this information was taken. That is, (1–14) refers to line 14 of Table 1 of the Source.

Table 14–5

Example for Chapter 14: Gross Savings and Investment Statement

	Debit	Credit
Fixed Investment		110.6
Change in Inventories		14.0
Depreciation	63.5	
Personal Savings	73.6	
Undistributed Profits	23.2	
Government Surplus	−36.1	
Net Foreign Investment	0.4	
Total	124.6	124.6

Table 14–6

United States Gross Savings and Investment Account, 1966, Derived from Table 14–4

	Debit Uses	Credit Sources
Gross Private Domestic Investment	118.0	
Net Foreign Investment	2.2	
Personal Savings		29.8
Undistributed Corporate Profits		27.8
Corporate Inventory Valuation Adjustment	1.6	
Capital Consumption Allowances		63.5
Government Surplus or Deficits, National Income and Product Accounts		3.2
Statistical Discrepancy		−2.6
Totals	121.8	121.8

vices. This implies that a zero value always appears for the national intermediate goods and that the net value of exports minus imports appears for the RW intermediate goods and services.

The statements for the nonproduction sectors basically reduce to the value of revenue as a credit, that of expenditures as a debit, and their difference as gross savings.

The NIP accounts for the United States in 1966, derived from Table 10–2, appear in Table 14–4.

14.3.2 *National Income and Product Identities*

The national income and product account is usually summarized in the identities

$$Y = C + I + X - M$$

and

$$Y = W + R + NP + T + DP$$

where Y = gross national product; C = consumption; I = gross investment; X = exports; M = imports; W = wages; R = rents, interest, and distributed profits; NP = nondistributed profits; T = taxes; and DP = depreciation.

The first of these identities represents the credit side of the production accounts in Table 14–2, while the second represents its debit side.

These identities play an important role in the construction of aggregated models.

14.4 Gross Savings and Investment Statement

The gross savings and investment statement is obtained from the consolidation of all the statements in the national income and product accounts. Those obtained from Tables 14–2 and 14–3 appear in Tables 14–5 and 14–6, respectively.

It should be observed that (except for the modification already explained of personal savings and undistributed profits) the upper part of Table 12–1 is a mirror reflection of Table 14–5. In the first table, savings and depreciation appear as credits (and are disaggregated by sector) while in Table 14–5 they appear as debits. Inversely, tangible assets appear in Table 12–1 as debits and in Table 14–5 as credits.

A point to be mentioned later is that, since all tangible assets are "controlled" by the production sector, investment in tangible assets is equal to undistributed profits plus depreciation.

15

Real and Financial Aspects of Economic Growth: Forecasting and Planning with Aggregated Models

15.1 Content of this Chapter

The main purpose of this chapter is to study the problems of economic planning when both real and financial variables are considered. To achieve this end, two aggregated models of growth will be used. These models are termed "aggregated" because it is assumed that only one multi-purpose "good" is produced by one multi-purpose "firm". In addition to this aggregated production sector, two other sectors will be considered: households and government, on one hand, and rest of the world, on the other.

15.2 The Simplest Model of Growth Integrating Real and Financial Aspects of the Economy

15.2.1 The Model

An extension of the Harrod-Domar model will be presented in this section. The purpose of this extension is to integrate the financial aspects of an economy with the real aspects. The latter have already been treated in the Harrod-Domar model.

An outline of the NTT to be used as a term of reference appears in Table 15–1. This table presents in symbols what Table 14–3 presented in numbers.

The set of endogenous variables in the model contains all the variables in Table 15–1. The method used to obtain the values of T_i' and B_i, once the values of I are given, was shown in Chapter 12. The values of DR_i and CR_i are obtained by aggregation. Thus, only the remaining 10 variables in Table 15–1 need to be considered here. Capital and gross national product, to be denoted by K and Y, respectively, will also be included among the endogenous variables. The values of all these variables for $t = 0$ are considered to be data.

The equations in the model are:

1. those presented in Section 12.3 to specify the values of all the variables in the FFS as a function of the vector of Tangible Assets.

Table 15–1
National Transactions Table to be Used in the Models in Sections 15.2 and 15.3

	Household and Government		Production		Rest of the World	
	Debit	Credit	Debit	Credit	Debit	Credit
Gross Savings		VH		NP		VRW
Investment Tangible Assets			I			
Capital Consumption				DP		
Financial Assets and Liabilities[a]	T'_1	B_1	T'_2	B_2	T'_3	B_3
Total Financial	DR_1	CR_1	DR_2	CR_2	DR_3	CR_3
Final Sales and Consumption	C			C		
Investment				I		
Exports				X		$-X$
Imports				$-M$		M
Depreciation			DP			
Wages, Rents, Profits, Interests		WR	WR			
Taxes		TX	TX			
Savings	VH		NP		VRW	

[a]The symbols T'_i, B_i denote the column vectors that form the matrices $[B]$ and $[T]$ in Table 12–3.

In particular, in Section 12.3, equations (12.2), (12.4), (12.10), and (12.14), it was shown that

$$[S] = [CR] - [C_{pj}]' [1]$$

$$[CR] = [DR] = [1 - D*C*]^{-1} [T]$$

$$[C_{jp}] = [C]* [\hat{C}R]$$

According to Table 15–1

$$[S]' = [VH, NP + DP, VRW]$$

$$[T]' = [0, 1, 0]I$$

Denoting with

$$[t_{ij}] = [1 - D*C*]^{-1}$$

and with the values that the t_{ij} have been given, it follows that

$$[CR]' = [t_{12}, t_{22}, t_{32}]I$$

so that

$$[S] = \{[t_{i2}] - [\hat{t}_{i2}][C^*]'[1]\}I \qquad (15.1)$$

This means that it is possible to write

$$VH_1 = f_1 I_1 \qquad (15.2)$$

$$NP_1 + DP_1 = f_2 I_1 \qquad (15.3)$$

$$VRW_1 = f_3 I_1 \qquad (15.4)$$

where the values of f_i are the constants obtained from the matrix coefficient of I in equation (15.1). Observe that since $VH + NP + DP + VRW = I$, it follows that the sum of the f_i is equal to 1.

2. the following accounting relationships:

$$Y_t = C_t + I_t + X_t - M_t \qquad (15.5)$$

$$Y_t = WR_t + NP_t + DP_t + TX_t \qquad (15.6)$$

$$WR_t = C_t + VH_t - TX_t \qquad (15.7)$$

$$VRW_t = M_t - X_t \qquad (15.8)$$

3. the following technical and behavioral expressions:

$$K_t = K_{t-1} - DP_{t-1} + I_{t-1} \qquad (15.9)$$

$$Y_t = \kappa K_t \qquad (15.10)$$

$$DP_t = \delta K_t \qquad (15.11)$$

$$C_t = c\,WR_t \qquad (15.12)$$

$$X_t = \epsilon X_{t-1} \qquad (15.13)$$

$$TX = 0 \qquad (15.14)$$

The system of equations included in the group numbered from (15.2) to (15.14) includes 13 equations. However, using the identity

$$I_t = VH_t + NP_t + DP_t + VRW_t$$

derived from the FFS and equations (15.6), (15.7), and (15.8), equation (15.5) can be obtained. This means that the system has no more than 12 independent equations.

15.2.2 Use of the Model for Forecasting

The method to be used for obtaining the values of the variables for period t, when those for $t-1$ are known, will be explained here.

The values of K_t, Y_t, DP_t, and X_t are obtained with equations (15.9), (15.10), (15.11), and (15.13). Next, with the system of equations including (15.2), (15.3), (15.6), (15.7), and (15.12), it can be shown that

$$I_t = (1-c)Y_t/[f_1 + (1-c)f_2] \qquad (15.15)$$

Once I_t is determined, the remaining variables in the income and product accounts are determined as follows:

$$VH_t \text{ with equation (15.2)}$$

$$NP_t \text{ with equation (15.3)}$$

$$VRW_t \text{ with equation (15.4)}$$

$$WR_t \text{ with equation (15.6)}$$

$$C_t \text{ with equation (15.7)}$$

$$M_t \text{ with equation (15.8)}$$

Finally, the variables in the FFS are determined using the method described in Section 12.2.

15.3 The Simplest Planning Model Integrating the Real and Financial Aspects of an Economy

15.3.1 The Model

To study the planning problem in its simplest terms, it will be assumed that a rate of growth for Y_t is adopted as a target. This target rate will be denoted here by g, and the target values of all the variables with a wave on top ($\sim$), for example, $\tilde{Y}$ is the target value of gross national product (GNP).

The introduction of a target rate of growth for Y is equivalent to the introduction of the equation

$$\tilde{Y}_{t+1} = gY_t \qquad (15.16)$$

The problem is to integrate equation (15.16) with the model in Section 15.2. To do this, it should be observed that $\tilde{Y}$ should replace Y. If this is done, the model consisting of that in Section 15.2 and equation (15.16) has more equations than endogenous variables, and as a result, since the equations are independent, the model is inconsistent.

To eliminate this problem, from a purely mathematical point of view either one equation in the model must be dropped or one variable must be added. The former approach will be used here.

The equation that is usually dropped is the consumption function in (15.12). The reason for this is that (according to the model being considered) in order to accelerate the rate of growth, real investment has to be increased, and, as a result, consumption has to be reduced.

In summary, the planning model is the same as the one in Section 15.2, with equation (15.12) excluded and equation (15.16) added.

15.3.2 Use of the Model for Planning

In using the model in Section 15.3.1 for planning purposes, it should be observed that the target values for date 1 cannot be achieved. The reason for this is that, fixing $\tilde{Y}_1$ with equation (15.16), $\tilde{K}_1$ and $\tilde{I}_0$ with equations (15.9) and (15.10), we find that the actual investment at date 0 is different from what is required at that date. As a result, the targets must be fixed for date 2.

Once the value of $\tilde{Y}_2$ is computed by means of a repeated application of equation (15.16), the following step should be taken: Evaluate by means of some rough approximation DP_1:

Compute $\quad \tilde{K}_1$ with equation (15.10)

Compute $\quad \tilde{I}_1$ with equation (15.9)

Compute $\quad \widetilde{VH}_1$ with equation (15.2)

Compute $\quad \widetilde{NP}_1$ with equation (15.3)

Compute $V\widetilde{R}W_1$ with equation (15.4)

Compute $\quad \widetilde{WR}_1$ with equation (15.6)

Compute $\quad \tilde{C}_1$ with equation (15.7)

Compute $\quad \tilde{X}_1$ with equation (15.13)

Compute $\quad \tilde{M}_1$ with equation (15.8)

Finally, the values of the variables in the FFS should be evaluated using the method in Section 12.2.

15.3.3 A Critique of the Model in Sections 15.3.1 and 15.3.2

The planning model just presented has two important limitations, which will be discussed here.

The first limitation is that it does not provide a link between the conditions of the economy at date 0 and those that are planned for dates $t = 1$, ..., T. When planning is introduced, a complete break with the past occurs. This is why the planning process has to start at date $t = 2$, and with an independent estimation of DP_1.

The second, and perhaps more serious, limitation of the model is that it does not show the effort needed to achieve the target values for GNP. This effort could be evaluated by the difference between the values that the variables should take in order to achieve the targets and those desired by the public in the economy being analyzed. This second set of values of the variables is determined with the model in Sections 15.2.1 and 15.2.2.

However, it should be observed that it is not enough to use the models in Sections 15.2 and 15.3 one at a time and then compute the differences between the values of the variables obtained with them. The reason for this is that if the economy actually reaches a target value for production, say on date 2, people would like to behave during the period between dates 2 and 3 in agreement with the target value achieved, and not in agreement with the conditions that the economy would have had without a plan, conditions that would be evaluated by forecasting with the value in Section 15.2. This means that, to eliminate the limitations of the planning model in Sections 15.3.1 and 15.3.2, a plan should be made which integrates the forecasting and the planning models presented. This will be done in Section 15.4.

15.4 Planning with the Ordered Use of the Models in Sections 15.2 and 15.3

The procedure to be used for planning with an ordered application of the models in Sections 15.2 and 15.3 will be explained in detail here. The notation introduced in previous sections will be used. In particular, the wave above a variable means that it is determined as a required value to achieve the target rate of growth.

As a starting point, the values for year 1 of the variables in the first model are computed, using the method in Section 15.2.1. The value of Y_1 is included among these.

Next, with the values of Y_1, g, and equation (15.14), the value of $\tilde{Y}_2$ is obtained. With this, the method in Section 15.3.2 can be used to estimate the values that the variables in the model should take in order to achieve $\tilde{Y}_2$. The only modification that should be considered in this method is that in computing $\tilde{I}_1$ with equation (15.9), the value of DP_1 computed with the model in Section 15.2 should be used. The independent estimate of DP_1 used in Section 15.3.2 is no longer required.

It follows from these observations that for all the variables with the exception of Y_1, DP_1, and X_1, two values are available for date 1: one forecasted using the method in Section 15.2.2 according to the conditions on date 0, and one required to achieve $\tilde{Y}_2$, computed with the method in Section 15.3.2. The difference between the required or target values of the variables and those forecasted specifies the adaptation needed in the economy between years 1 and 2 in order to achieve the targets for date 2.

Next, it is assumed that the required values of the variables have actually been reached in period 1. This provides a starting point for using the model in Section 15.2 to forecast the economy to date 2. Again, the value of Y_2 is used to compute $\tilde{Y}_3$ and to initiate the computation of the required values of the variables at date 2.

The process of alternately forecasting and planning is repeated until the whole planning horizon is covered.

15.5 An Extention of the Basic Model

15.5.1 The Model for Forecasting

In this section, the model in Section 15.2 will be extended to include the use of raw materials in the production process. A more detailed analysis of national and imported goods will also be made. The assumption that the economy produces only one good, used both for consumption as a raw material and for investment, will be retained. This assumption will be relaxed, however, in Chapter 16, in which a disaggregated model of economic growth is presented. This disaggregated model is an immediate generalization of the one to be presented here.

The principal variables in the model and the accounting identities among them are presented in Table 15–2. This table presents in symbols what Table 14–3 presented in numbers.

As in Section 15.1, and for the same reasons, no attention will be paid to T_i^1, B_i, DR_i, and CR_i. To complete the set of endogenous variables in the model, 6 variables must be added. They will be presented later. The model has a total of 20 endogenous variables. As before, the values of all these variables for $t = 0$ are considered to be predetermined.

In order to link the variables in Table 15–2 with the accounting identities in Section 15.2.1 (part 2), the following obvious definitions will be used:

$$C_t = CN_t + CM_t \tag{15.17}$$

$$I_t = IN_t + IM_t \tag{15.18}$$

Table 15–2
National Transactions Table to be Used in the Model in Section 15.5

	Households		Production		Rest of the World	
	Debit	Credit	Debit	Credit	Debit	Credit
Gross Savings		VH		NP		VRW
Investment Tangible Assets			I			
Capital Consumption				DP		
Financial Assets and Liabilities[a]	T'_1	B_1	T'_2	B_2	T'_3	V_3
Total Financial	DR_1	CR_1	DR_2	CR_2	SR_3	CR_3
HL Final Consumption	CN			CN		
RW Final Consumption	CM		CM	CM		CM
HL Intermediate Goods			DN	DN		
RW Intermediate Goods			DM	X	X	DM
HL Capital Goods				IN		
RW Capital Goods			IM	IM		IM
Depreciation			DP			
Wages, Rents, Profits, Interests		WR	WR			
Taxes		TX	TX			
Savings	VH		NP		VRW	

[a]See note for Table 15–1.

that is, the totals of consumption and investment are equal to national plus imported.

For imports we have

$$M_t = CM_t + IM_t + DM_t \qquad (15.19)$$

With these definitions, it is clear that

$$Y_t = C_t + I_t + X_t - M_t \qquad (15.20)$$

as in Section 15.2.1.

The remaining identities in equations (15.6) through (15.8) are still valid. These identities are

$$Y_t = WR_t + NP_t + DP_t + TX_t \qquad (15.21)$$

$$WR_t = C_t + VH_t - TX_t \qquad (15.22)$$

$$VRW_t = M_t - X_t \qquad (15.23)$$

The following variables and identities will also be used:

$$E_t = CN_t + IN_t + X_t \qquad (15.24)$$

that is, E_t is the total of national goods in final uses.

$$P_t = E_t + DN_t \qquad (15.25)$$

where P_t is total national production.

Several relationships can be derived from the accounting identities and definitions given here. Those that will be used in the model in this section will now be presented.

It follows from equations (15.17) through (15.20) that

$$Y_t = CN_t + IN_t + X_t - DM_t \qquad (15.26)$$

and from equations (15.24) and (15.26) that

$$Y_t = E_t - DM_t \qquad (15.27)$$

From equations (15.25) and (15.27) it also follows that

$$P_t = Y_t + DN_t + DM_t \qquad (15.28)$$

that is, as would be expected, total production including raw materials (P_t) is equal to production excluding raw materials (Y_t) plus raw materials ($DN_t + DM_t$).

All the endogenous variables and accounting relationships in the model have been presented, and the behavioral and technical equations will now be introduced.

First, as in the case of the model in Section 15.2.1, the relationship presented in Section 12.2 that makes it possible to specify all the variables in the FFS once the value of tangible assets is specified will be included in the following model. In particular, equations (15.2) to (15.4) will be used in this section.

Next, the following straightforward adaptation of equation (15.5) to (15.10) will be used:

$$K_t = K_{t-1} - DP_{t-1} + I_{t-1} \qquad (15.29)$$

$$DP_t = \delta K_t \qquad (15.30)$$

$$P_t = \kappa K_t \qquad (15.31)$$

$$C_t = cWR_t \qquad (15.32)$$

$$X_t = \epsilon X_{t-1} \qquad (15.33)$$

$$TX = 0 \qquad (15.34)$$

Finally, the following technical relationships will be used:

$$DN_t = \alpha P_t \qquad (15.35)$$

$$DM_t = \eta P_t \qquad (15.36)$$

and

$$IM_t = \mu I_t \qquad (15.37)$$

The model presented has a total of 24 equations. However, equations (15.21) to (15.23) and the identity

$$I_t = VH_t + NP_t + DP_t + VRW_t$$

imply equation (15.20). Second, equation (15.26) follows from equations (15.17) to (15.20). The same is true for equation (15.27), which follows from equations (15.24) and (15.26). Finally, equations (15.25) and (15.27) imply equation (15.28). This shows that the system has at most 20 independent equations.

15.5.2 Use of the Model for Forecasting

The following procedure can be used to compute the values of the variables for date 1, when those for date t are known:

1. Use equation (15.29) to compute K_1
2. Use equation (15.30) to compute DP_1
3. Use equation (15.31) to compute P_1
4. Use equation (15.35) to compute DN_1
5. Use equation (15.36) to compute DM_1
6. Use equation (15.25) to compute E_1
7. Use equation (15.27) to complete Y_1
8. Use equation (15.33) to compute X_1

Next the system of equations formed by equations (15.2) and (15.3) and by equations (15.21), (15.22), and (15.32) is used to obtain $I = (i-c) Y/[f_1 + (i-c)f_2]$ and the values of WR_1, NP_1, C_1, VH_1, and I_1.

1. Use equation (15.37) to compute IM_1
2. Use equation (15.18) to compute IN_1
3. Use equation (15.26) to compute CN_1
4. Use equation (15.17) to compute CM_1
5. Use equation (15.19) to compute M_1
6. Use equation (15.23) to compute VRW_1

It might seem surprising that VRW is computed from equation (15.23) instead of from equation (15.4), which would seem to be the more direct method. The reason for this is that the method just given can be adapted to the models in Chapter 16. It should be observed, however, that the value of VRW computed with equation (15.4) enters the model through the NTT identity and shows that equation (15.20) is not independent. As a result, the value of VRW derived here and that which could be obtained with equation (15.20) must be the same.

15.5.3 Planning with the Model in Section 15.5.1

To transform the model in Section 15.5.1 into a planning model, the method used in Section 15.3 will be employed again. In the present case, the consumption function in equation (15.32) is replaced with a target-setting function

$$\tilde{Y}_{t+1} = g Y_t \qquad (15.38)$$

The application of only the model just described to planning will not be presented here. Instead, the use of both the forecasting model in Sections 15.5.1 and 15.5.2 and the planning model just described will be presented. The method follows quite closely that presented in Section 15.4.

First, the method in Section 15.5.2 is used to forecast the values of all the variables for date $t = 0$ to date $t = 1$. This step shows that even if we assume that the economy is still at date $t = 0$, the values of P_1, DP_1, DN_1, DM_1, E_1, Y_1, X_1, and K_1 are not under the control of the planners. In order to achieve the targets for $t = 0$, all the planners can do is modify the values of the other variables. Basically, this means to modify the distribution between consumption and investment.

Once the forecast to determine $t = 1$ is completed, equation (15.38) is used to evaluate $\tilde{Y}_2$.

The values of $\tilde{P}_2$, $\tilde{DN}_2$, and $\tilde{DM}_2$ are obtained with the system of equations formed with (15.28), (15.35), and (15.36).

Equation (15.31) is used to obtain $\tilde{K}_2$; equation (15.29) and the forecasted values of K_1 and DP_1 are used to evaluate $\tilde{I}_1$.

Next the following sequence of operations is used:

1. With equation (15.2) the value of $\tilde{VH}_1$ is obtained
2. With equation (15.3) the value of $\tilde{NP}_1$ is obtained
3. With equation (15.4) the value of VRW_1 is obtained
4. With equation (15.5) the value of $\tilde{WR}_1$ is obtained
5. With equation (15.22) the value of $\tilde{C}_1$ is obtained
6. With equation (15.23) the value of $\tilde{M}_1$ is obtained
7. With equation (15.37) the value of $\tilde{IM}_1$ is obtained
8. With equation (15.18) the value of $\tilde{IN}_1$ is obtained.

Finally, the values of $C\widetilde{N}_1$ and $C\widetilde{M}_1$ are obtained from the system formed by equations (15.17) and (15.19).

It is useful to verify that the values determined with the forecast from date $t = 0$ only still hold true. To do so, it should be observed that from the identities of the NTT it follows that

$$V\widetilde{H}_1 + \widetilde{NP}_1 + DP_1 + S\widetilde{R}W_1 = \tilde{I}_1 \tag{15.39}$$

Also, from the method of computation of $\widetilde{W}R_1$ it follows that the forecasted value of Y_1 is maintained, that is, the equation

$$Y_1 = \widetilde{WR}_1 + \widetilde{NP}_1 + \widetilde{DP}_1$$

holds.

Since equation (15.22) is used to evaluate $\tilde{C}_1$, the preceding equation can be written

$$Y_1 = \tilde{C}_1 + V\widetilde{H}_1 + \widetilde{NP}_1 + DP_1 \tag{15.40}$$

Finally, with equations (15.23), (15.39), and (15.40) it can be shown that

$$Y_1 = \tilde{C}_1 + \tilde{I}_1 + \tilde{X}_1 - \tilde{M}_1.$$

The fact that the values of P_1, DN_1, and DM_1 are consistent with the required values to achieve the targets for $t = 2$ follows from equations (15.28), (15.35), and (15.36).

No verification is needed with respect to the forecasted values used as data in the estimation of the values required to achieve the targets.

Reference

Herzog, Philippe, and Vajda, Pierre, "Esquisse d'un modele de projection macro-economique integrant des variables financiers," *Annales de l'Insee* (May 1969).

16
Real and Financial Aspects of Economic Growth: Forecasting and Planning with Interindustry Models

16.1 The Model

The model presented in Section 15.5 is extended here to include the assumption that the economy produces and imports several types of goods and services, all of which are used for consumption as raw materials or for investment.

In the model, n production sectors will be considered. As a result, most of the variables in Section 15.5.1 should have a subscript by sector. To simplify presentation, matrix notation will be used. A matrix will be denoted by the symbol for the components of the matrix surrounded by square brackets. In addition, next to the matrix equations the number of linear equations represented by the matrix equation will be indicated. The total over all sectors will be considered for some variables. They will be denoted in most cases with an S in front of the name of the variable.

The accounting identities in equations (15.17) to (15.21) and (15.24) to (15.28) can be written immediately, replacing each of the variables appearing in them with a matrix of n rows and 1 column. On the other hand, there is no basis for subdividing the savings of households or of rest of the world by sectors. As a result, equations (15.22) and (15.23) are valid only for the national totals.

With the observation made, the accounting identities in equations (15.17) to (15.28) take the following forms:

$$[C]_t = [CN]_t + [CM]_t \qquad (n \text{ eq}) \qquad (16.1)$$

$$[I]_t = [IN]_t + [IM]_t \qquad (n \text{ eq}) \qquad (16.2)$$

$$[M]_t = [CM]_t + [IM]_t + [DM]_t \qquad (n \text{ eq}) \qquad (16.3)$$

$$[Y]_t = [C]_t + [I]_t + [X]_t - [M]_t \qquad (n \text{ eq}) \qquad (16.4)$$

$$[Y]_t = [WR]_t + [NP]_t + [DP]_t \qquad (n \text{ eq}) \qquad (16.5)$$

$$SWR_t = SC_t + VH_t \qquad (1 \text{ eq}) \qquad (16.6)$$

$$VRW_t = SM_t - SX_t \qquad (1 \text{ eq}) \qquad (16.7)$$

$$[E]_t = [CN]_t + [IN]_t + [X]_t \qquad (n \text{ eq}) \qquad (16.8)$$

$$[P]_t = [E]_t + [DN]_t \qquad (n \text{ eq}) \qquad (16.9)$$

$$[Y]_t = [CN]_t + [IN]_t + [X]_t - [DM]_t \qquad (n \text{ eq}) \qquad (16.10)$$

$$[Y]_t = [E]_t - [DM]_t \qquad (n \text{ eq}) \qquad (16.11)$$

$$[P]_t = [Y]_t + [DN]_t + [DM]_t \qquad (n \text{ eq}) \qquad (16.12)$$

Equations (15.29) and (15.30) are disaggregated as follows:

$$[KN_{ij}]_t = [\sigma_i KN_{ij}]_{t-1} + [IN_{ij}]_{t-1} \qquad (n^2 \text{ eq}) \qquad (16.13\text{A})$$

$$[KM_{ij}]_t = [\sigma_i KM_{ij}]_{t-1} + [IM_{ij}]_{t-1} \qquad (n^2 \text{ eq}) \qquad (16.13\text{B})$$

$$[K_{ij}]_t = [KN_{ij}]_t + [KM_{ij}]_t \qquad (n^2 \text{ eq}) \qquad (16.13\text{C})$$

$$[DP_i]_t = [(1 - \sigma_i)K_{ij}]_t[1] \qquad (n \text{ eq}) \qquad (16.14)$$

where KN_{ij} is the stock of national good j used as capital by industry i, that is, the matrix $[KN_{ij}]$ has n^2 components. IN_{ij} is the investment in national goods j by industry i. The respective matrix has n^2 components. $(1 - \sigma_i)$ is the depreciation rate for capital goods in industry i. It is assumed that all goods used as capital in industry i depreciate at the same rate. [1] is a column vector with only ones as components. The meanings of the other symbols should be clear.

The production function in equation (15.31) will be replaced here with

$$P_{it} = \min(\kappa v_{ij} KN_{ijt} \kappa \mu_{ij} KM_{ijt}) \qquad (16.15)$$

where κv_{ij} is the amount of good i that can be produced with a stock of one unit of national good j used as capital when all the other goods used as capital are insufficient or in oversupply. The definition of $\kappa \mu_{ij}$ is similar.

When a national good, say, h, is not used as capital in the production of good i, the coefficient κv_{ij} is assumed to be infinity. A similar statement is valid for an imported good. As a result, the range of j in equation (16.15) should be restricted to the goods that are used as capital in the production of i.

In equation (16.15), complementarity is assumed among the different goods used as capital. This is equivalent to assuming that the different capital goods perform specialized functions in the production process, a hypothesis that seems more reasonable than its opposite, that is, that any good can perform all functions in the production process.

The remaining equations in Section 15.5.1 can be adapted with only minor modifications. They take the following forms:

$$[C]_t = [c]SWR_t \qquad (n \text{ eq}) \qquad (16.16)$$

$$[X]_t = [\hat{\epsilon}]^a[X]_{t-1} \qquad (n \text{ eq}) \qquad (16.17)$$

---

[a] $[\hat{\epsilon}]$ is a matrix with the rates of growth of the X_i in the main diagonal and zeros everywhere else.

$$[TX] = 0 \qquad (n \text{ eq}) \qquad (16.18)$$

$$[DN]_t = [\alpha][P]_t \qquad (n \text{ eq}) \qquad (16.19)$$

$$[DM]_t = [\eta][P]_t \qquad (n \text{ eq}) \qquad (16.20)$$

$$IM_{ij} = \mu_{ij} IN_{ij} \qquad (n^2 \text{ eq}) \qquad (16.21)$$

In addition to the equations introduced so far, those derived from the analysis of the FFS must be used, that is,

$$VH_t = [f_1][I]_t \qquad (1 \text{ eq}) \qquad (16.22)$$

$$[NP_t + DP_t] = [f_2][I]_t \qquad (n \text{ eq}) \qquad (16.23)$$

$$VRW_t = [f_3][I]_t \qquad (1 \text{ eq}) \qquad (16.24)$$

In these equations the vector $[I]$ has as components the tangible investment of all sectors of the economy, including, in addition to the production sector, households and rest of the world. As in Section 15.1, it will be assumed that investment in tangible assets by households and rest of the world is zero. As a result, the vector $[I]_t$ in equations (16.22) to (16.24) has the first component equal to zero, components 2 to $n+1$ equal to the vector I in equation (16.4), and an $n+2$ component again equal to zero. The matrices $[f_i]$ have the appropriate dimensions and are derived with the method presented in Section 15.2.1.

Finally, the following totals will be used:

$$IN_i = \sum_j IN_{ij} \qquad (n \text{ eq}) \qquad (16.25)$$

$$IM_i = \sum_j IM_{ij} \qquad (n \text{ eq}) \qquad (16.26)$$

$$SWR = [1]'[WR] \qquad (1 \text{ eq}) \qquad (16.27)$$

$$SC = [1]'[C] \qquad (1 \text{ eq}) \qquad (16.28)$$

$$SM = [1]'[M] \qquad (1 \text{ eq}) \qquad (16.29)$$

$$SX = [1]'[X] \qquad (1 \text{ eq}) \qquad (16.30)$$

The system has $4n^2 + 19n + 8$ equations plus the relationship in equation (16.15) that will be replaced with a system of $2n^2$ inequalities. However, these inequalities cannot be assumed to determine the values of any variables.

The equations in the system just given are not independent. As in the case of equation (15.1), equation (16.4) can be derived from equations (16.1), (16.2), (16.3), and (16.10); equations (16.12) from equations (16.9) and (16.11); equation (16.11) from equations (16.8) and (16.10); that is, so far it has been shown that $3n$ equations are not independent.

The following relationship among totals can also be established:
From equation (16.4) we obtain

$$SY_t = SC_t + SI_t + SX_t - SM_t$$

From equation (16.5) we obtain

$$SY_t = SWR_t + SNP_t + SDP_t$$

and these two relations, together with equations (16.6), (16.7), (16.24), and

$$SI_t = VH_t + SNP_t + SDP_t + VRW_t$$

do not form an independent system. As a result, one of the equations (16.7) or (16.24) can be eliminated from the system.

In summary, the system has at most $4n^2 + 16n + 7$ independent equations.

On the other hand, it can be shown that the number of variables in the system is $5n^2 + 17n + 6$. This means that the number of variables is larger than that of equations. The system is not determined. To apply it for forecasting or planning, either additional equations must be added, or an optimization process must be used. The latter approach will be used here.

16.2 Use of the Model in Forecasting

As observed, the model in Section 16.1 is not complete. It cannot be used to forecast the evolution of the economy from one year to another.

One reason for this is that no mechanism to allocate investment among the different production processes is included in the model. One alternative for this is to assume that the total amount of nonconsumed goods of type j is distributed among the different production processes in proportion to the values of K_{ij}, that is, in proportion to the amount of capital of type j already in use in sector i. With this assumption, or any similar to it, no attention is paid to the fact that investment is actually allocated in agreement with the characteristics of final demand and the technology of production, rather than as determined by past trends. It is known that the allocation according to past trends causes unstable models.

In actual practice the allocation of investment among the different production processes is made in such a way as to maximize profits. This is the automatic effect of the market mechanism.

In a model, in order to take into considereation the characteristics of final demand and technology, the allocation of investment must also be made with an optimization process. This process will now be explained.

As a first step, the following maximization will now be considered: Maximize

$$Z_1 = [1]'[Y]_{t+1}$$

subject to

$$P_{it} + 1 \le \kappa \nu_{ij} KN_{ijt+1} \qquad (16.15\text{A})$$

$$P_{it} + 1 \le \kappa \mu_{ij} KM_{ijt+1} \qquad (16.15\text{B})$$

and equations (16.12), (16.13A), (16.13B), (16.19), (16.20), (16.21), for date $t+1$ and (16.2), (16.25), and (16.26) for date t.

Clearly, the object of this model is to distribute the total tangible investment of industry among investments in goods produced by sector j, $j = 1, \ldots, n$.

The optimization process just described uses $3n^2 + 6n$ equations plus $2n^2$ inequalities, and determines the values of the following $4n^2 + 6n$ variables: $KN_{ijt+1}(n^2)$, $KM_{ijt+1}(n^2)$, $IM_{ijt}(n^2)$, $IN_{ijt}(n^2)$, $IM_{it}(n)$, $IN_{it}(n)$, $Y_{t+1}(n)$, $P_{t+1}(n)$, $DN_{t+1}(n)$, and $DM_{t+1}(n)$.

Next, the values of K_{ijt+1} and DP_{it+1} can be determined with equations (16.13C) and (16.14). This uses $n^2 + n$ equations and determines the same number of variables.

At this stage it can be shown that the number of equations $(10n + 7)$ is still less than that of unknowns $(12n + 6)$. A new optimization process must be used. At this point the problem is to distribute the goods available at date $t+1$ between consumption and investment. For this, maximize

$$Z_2 = \sum_i \text{coef}_{1i} C_i + \sum \text{coef}_{2i} I_i$$

subject to equations (16.5), (16.6), (16.16), (16.22), (16.23), (16.27), and (16.28), all with respect to date $t+1$.

The parameters coef_{1i} and coef_{2i} in the objective function are indices of the utility provided to society by the consumption or the investment of one unit of good i. The estimation of these parameters presents serious methodological and informational problems. For this reason, the following procedure is suggested:

Replace the objective function with

$$Z_3 = p \sum C_i + (1-p) \sum I_i$$

that is, assume that the consumption of any good produces the same satisfaction as the consumption of any other good, and also that the investment of any one good produces the same satisfaction as the investment of another. With Z_3 only one parameter has to be evaluated.

To evaluate p, a sequence of values of p should be used, and for each p, the values obtained with the model for all the variables should be recorded. Then these recorded values should be compared with the actual ones. The value of p for which the difference between estimated and actual values of the variables is a minimum should be used as the estimate of the actual p for a society.

The optimization of Z_3 uses $3n + 4$ equations and determines $4n + 3$ variables $WR_{t+1}(n)$, $NP_{t+1}(n)$, $C_{t+1}(n)$, $VH_{t+1}(1)$, $I_{t+1}(n)$, $SWR_{t+1}(1)$, and $SC_{t+1}(1)$.

The remaining system includes equations (16.1), (16.3), (16.4), (16.7), (16.8), (16.9), (16.10), (16.11), (16.17), (16.18), (16.24), (16.29), and (16.30), that is, a total of $9n + 4$ equations. It has been shown that 3 sets of n equations each, plus one of 1 equation, are dependent, that is, the system includes at most $6n + 3$ independent equations. The variables in the system are the following $6n + 3$: $CN(n)$, $CM(n)$, $M(n)$, $X(n)$, $E(n)$, $TX(n)$, $VRW(1)$, $SM(1)$, and $SX(1)$. That is, the system of equations can be used to determine the values of the unknowns. For this, the following procedure can be used:

1. With equation (16.17) evaluate X_i $i = 1, \ldots, n$
2. With equation (16.10) evaluate CN_i, $i = 1, \ldots, n$
3. With equation (16.1) evaluate CM_i, $i = 1, \ldots, n$
4. With equation (16.3) evaluate M_i, $i = 1, \ldots, n$
5. With equation (16.29) evaluate SM
6. With equation (16.30) evaluate SX
7. With equation (16.7) evaluate VRW
8. With equation (16.8) evaluate E_i, $i = 1, \ldots, n$
9. With equation (16.18) evaluate TX_i, $i = 1, \ldots, n$

16.3 Use of the Model for Planning

Again, in this case, a combination of forecasting and "pure" planning procedures will be used. The procedure will be explained, using as an example the determination of the required values at date $t=1$, when the forecast for date $t=1$ from year zero is ready, and the target for $\widetilde{SY}$ at date $t=2$ has been fixed. As before, this target is fixed with equation

$$\widetilde{SY}_{t+1} = gSY_t \tag{16.31}$$

where

$$SY_t = [1]'[Y]_t \tag{16.32}$$

It will be assumed that the object of the planning process is, in the present case, to minimize the investment needed to achieve the targets, that is, to minimize

$$Z_4 = [1]'[\tilde{I}]_1$$

subject to equations (16.2), (16.21), (16.25), and (16.26) with respect to date t, and (16.12), (16.13A), (16.13B), (16.15A), (16.15B), (16.19), (16.20), and (16.31) and (16.32) with respect to date $t+1$. This minimization determines the values of the same variables as the maximization in Section 16.2 and, in addition, those of $[\tilde{I}]$.

To continue, observe that $[DP]_1$ is determined in the forecasting part of the process. Next, the following procedure should be used:

1. With equation (16.22) evaluate $[\widetilde{VH}]_1$
2. With equation (16.23) evaluate $[\widetilde{NP}]_1$
3. With equation (16.5) evaluate $[\widetilde{WR}]_1$
4. With equation (16.27) evaluate $S\widetilde{WR}$
5. With equation (16.16) evaluate $[\tilde{C}]_1$
6. With equation (16.20) evaluate $\widetilde{SC}_1$

It should be observed that with the determination of the values of $[I]_i$, the possibility of choice for the consumers has been eliminated, that is, there is no possibility of an optimization process.

The remaining required values of the variables are determined with the method used to compute the forecasted values with the model in Section 15.2. The details will not be repeated here.

17 Concluding Remarks

This book was begun as an attempt to find a logically consistent basis for macro-accounting. It soon became clear that this would be possible only if macro-accounting were presented as the result of aggregating and consolidating the micro-accounts in an economy. It is to be hoped that the results presented in the previous chapters are a more esthetic presentation of macro-accounting.

As an immediate consequence of the integration of micro- and macro-accounting, the need appeared to treat more fully the financial aspects of the economy, and to better integrate them with the real aspects. The results presented in the previous chapters, in particular the generalized equation of exchange, should improve the integration of real and monetary aspects in the analysis of the economic processes.

It should be observed at this point that the analysis of the properties of the generalized equation of exchange and the possibility of using it in the study of the economic processes are still at a very early stage of development. Perhaps research on these topics will open up new ways to understand the economic processes, and will provide new instruments for policy making.

Perhaps in a more remote way, this book suggests that accounting in general, and micro-accounting particularly, should be better integrated with economic theory. It is somewhat surprising that micro-accounting has been very little used by economists as a basis for gaining additional insight into the economic processes. At this stage it is possible to suggest avenues of research that seem to promise fruitful results. These avenues could be briefly described as follows. Accounting identities, particularly what has been called here the transaction equation, could be used as the constraints that are frequently introduced in micro-economic theory as limiting the behavior of economic units. It can be shown that the use of these new constraints, without modifying the basic methods of analysis, makes it possible to introduce money into the analysis of the behavior of households, firms (industrial or financial), and so forth. With this basis, it is possible to construct a micro-economic theory that is more appealing from an intuitive point of view; that is, a micro-economic theory in which the role of money is taken into full consideration. In addition, following very closely the classical lines of economic analysis, it is possible to improve general economic equilibrium, introducing money again in a simpli-

215

fied way to that type of analysis. In this approach, the national transactions table appears as an expression of the general economic equilibrium.

It is hoped that the research possibilities mentioned here will attract the attention of economists at least to the point of verifying whether the statements made provide a basis for the suggested extension of economic theory.

Index

Index

219

About the Author

Hector Correa, a native of Ecuador, has been an associate professor in the Graduate School of Public and International Affairs at the University of Pittsburgh since 1970. After completing studies in social sciences, economics, and mathematics at the Universidad Central del Ecuador, he recieved the M.S. in mathematics from the University of Kansas, the Ph.D. in mathematical economics from the Netherlands School of Economics in Rotterdam. A consultant to several governments, Professor Correa has also worked for several branches of the United Nations, including the International Labor Office, FAO, UNESCO, U.N. Headquarters, and UNICEF. He is the author of five books, several monographs, and numerous journal articles dealing with economics, education, health, nutrition, population, and social sciences in general.